IF SOME OF YOUR BEST FRIENDS ARE HOB-BITS. . .

IF YOU'D RATHER VISIT MIDDLE-EARTH THAN DISNEYLAND. . .

THIS IS YOUR BOOK!

"Coming years will produce a growing library of criticism and biography about J. R. R. Tolkien and his writings. However . . . we doubt that any of them will ever excel William Ready's brief critical appreciation in depth and sensitivity of perception into the meanings of Professor Tolkien's *The Lord of the Rings* trilogy, which he calls 'the masterpiece of imaginative and spiritual literature.' "
—*Chicago Daily News*

THE ONLY GUIDE TO TOLKIEN'S WORLD AVAILABLE IN AMERICA!

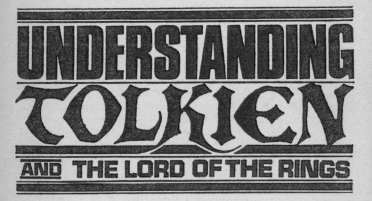

UNDERSTANDING TOLKIEN
AND THE LORD OF THE RINGS

(Original title: The Tolkien Relation)
by WILLIAM READY

WARNER

PAPERBACK LIBRARY
NEW YORK

WARNER PAPERBACK LIBRARY EDITION

First Printing: January, 1969
Second Printing: May, 1969
Third Printing: December, 1971
Fourth Printing: January, 1973

Cover illustration by Stan Zagorski

Warner Paperback Library is a division of Warner Books, Inc., 315 Park Avenue South, New York, N.Y. 10010.

CONTENTS

I	The Early Circle	7
II	The Inklings and the Myth	19
III	The Days of the Dons	33
IV	The Hobbits of Tolkien	42
V	The Tale of the Ring	53
VI	Craft and Art	58
VII	Man for Tolkien	62
VIII	The Once and the Future	72
IX	As It Was and Will Be	85
X	Epilogue	92

LORE

WIZARD

TOLKIEN

HOBBITS

PHROPHET

SHIRE

CHAPTER I

THE EARLY CIRCLE

Tolkien is a man full of *lore*, a word that fits Tolkien like the skin of the hand the sinews, bones and blood of it. The word implies that it can be taught, and also counsel and learning, scholarship, erudition, guile and more—the marks of a wizard. All the attributes of lore are in Tolkien. Herbert Merritt, Professor of Philology at Stanford, used the lore word well when he used it to describe Tolkien.

John Ronald Reuel Tolkien belongs first of all to the world of philologists, those who love words set down in proper and basic style to reveal what lies beyond —Humanity and Order. The Word and the root of it are in the beginning of any relation to Tolkien. Yet, above all, Tolkien is a prophet in a mist in a mask, a chronicler of Time and Earth, of Hobbits. The mask is in his being; the mist, the exhalation of Man. He does not divine, nor is there worship anywhere in his books. He does not create; he subcreates. He is a man of lore who makes sense by nonsense and relates it after a life and learning so skillfully that it all becomes one; no breaks occur in his tales to snag the reader's mind, although there are many irritations and imperfections of content and of style, some bland and eyeless disregard of facts of life, of the poor, of the beauty that passes and is the more lovely so, a lack of sensuality and humor. Yet truth enters in, carefully concocted in heroic significance, the Tolkien brew. Life takes on a full dimension. He tells that Man can inherit and hold the earth for a while, in danger always, in tribulation often; that if he wills it, he can relate with all that is good in nature and beyond. But Man falters often, so that there is apprehension ever in his tale, and Time is the enemy, ever on Evil's side.

Tolkien never blinks this heroic theme, never again after *The Hobbit*, save in little pieces, demeans it to his listeners, be they children, by chortling or lisping the words of it. It is a theme he has lived with all his life, since his first early days near the high veld town with the lovely and prophetic name of Bloemfontein, now one of the three capital cities of South Africa, where he was born in 1892. His father was a bank manager, son of a well-established family that had come to England from Saxony generations before and had become as English as Hereford or Avon.

In 1892 Bloemfontein was a pleasant, remote pioneer settlement with peace around, and yet with a stirring of awful things to come, which were to lead to the beginning of the end of the ordered days. *Pax Britannica* was through, over and done with, turned into a zombie by the flourishes of skirmishes, sieges, battles and concentration camps that were to become inexorable as doom, as a blight on the West before the next century was half over. It was such a time as Tolkien describes in *The Fellowship of the Ring*, the first book of his Trilogy, *The Lord of the Rings*.

The Hobbits, whom he had first created in a children's tale, *The Hobbit*, had pioneered their way to the Shire, overland across the Misty Mountains in the East, from the shade of Mirkwood, where once they had flourished under the trees that once had been Greenwood the Great. They had crossed the brown river of Baranduin and passed over the Bridge of Stonebows to make their lasting habitation the Shire, the Shire of Tolkien's Land that perhaps never was but like the Forest of Arden ever will be in bemused English eyes, which can see through mist, from behind a mask. There the Hobbits lived under the faint, distant and failing rule of the Dúnedain men, spoke in Westron, the Dúnedain tongue, and in return for their land kept the bridges and roads in repair and respected messengers of the high king at Fornost.

The land was at peace when the tale begins, crops abounded, the Hobbits were contented—it did not take much to content them, no more than little people anywhere—turning their backs and minds away from the dark things beyond their snug, dull, mock-rural bit of a world.

8

Unease was rising outside the Shire, rumors and incidents, but the Hobbits snuggled down all the more, wanting no part of it. Elves were moving westward toward the Sea of Westernesse, more dwarves than ever were hurrying out along the East-West Road. There were whispers of the arising of the Dark Enemy; it was like a shadow of all night falling, like a final evening of a day that had shone with sun too long to last. There were wars, rumors of wars. Trolls were abroad. Now, as the story goes, the trolls, elves, dwarves, orcs, all the rest become easy to see in the story, and it would have been better so, without the footnotes and fake history, the interminable appendices that litter the flow of the tale and are the cause of most of the trouble that daily flutters in letters around Tolkien; he brought this on himself but could no more reject it than he could have avoided starting it.

His mother had tales to tell from her strange past. Before her marriage, Mabel Suffield had worked with her sisters as a missionary among the women of the Sultan of Zanzibar. When he was but a little child, Tolkien was snatched away by a black servant, who wanted to show the lad off in his kraal. (Tolkien is a bluff and hearty know-nothing when it comes to blacks: fine chaps perhaps in their place, surely with immortal souls, but not in England. His views are shared by many of his kind and age.)

Concerning those baby days of his life, he said to an inquiring reporter, "I was nearly bitten by a snake and I was stung by a tarantula, I believe. In my garden. All I can remember is a very hot day, long dead grass and running. I don't even remember screaming." Really, he left Africa at such an early age—before he was four—there is not much he could remember.

He was taken away from the blaze of his African life when he was very young, for his health: he was a sickly child, and he never saw his father, who died a year later, again. His mother returned with him and his brother, who became an apple farmer, to a village near his father's native Birmingham in 1896, to the safety of the inmost Shire. Birmingham, in Warwickshire, is the town of all of England that is farthest from the sea, where the troubles always come from, the sea that is England's moat, the fishy deep whence came the Phoenicians to trade, the Romans to establish order, the Norse to batter and later to rule, the sea that was to enter the bloodstream of England and make her what she has become, more than an Island, an Idea, a Vision that none beyond the sea could share, nor ever will, and there is the trouble with any understanding of Tolkien.

Another hemisphere—the place where I belonged but which was totally novel and strange. After the barren, arid heat a Christmas tree. But no, it was not an unhappy childhood. It was full of tragedies but it didn't tot up to an unhappy childhood.

Tolkien related this memory of coming home in an interview more than sixty years later, and he left it at that: it was enough. The tragedies, if tragedies they were, are locked deep in Tolkien, save one, and that is a great one: the loss of his father, a blow to a boy against which he must fend for himself at whatever cost. Tolkien is sure of this and says it, in other ways, in detesting adultery, for instance, in defending the rulers of the Church, God's law to him, about the sanctity of marriage, the keeping of promises.

The death of his father, his uprooting from his birthplace in the Orange Free State and his sickliness were enough for any boy to bear. There was a bitter-sweet poignancy of those days in England before the first Great War, a jollity, a flare that presaged the dying of England's day. This was felt especially among the bourgeois but extended down even among the poor, whose lot was slowly improving, although the working poor are a people that fall outside Tolkien's ken. He was to know enough of genteel poverty, and that often is more scouring of the spirit. His mother became his teacher, and the quiet kindness of the English air around Sarehole, the Warwickshire village in the countryside in which Shakespeare wandered as a boy, was a balm that salved but never healed. He delved in England, in the pleasant rural place where he lived his rather solitary childhood under his mother's care—it was from his mother, he remembers, that sprang his love for romance and philology.

10

The traumatic shock of his father's death and of his own departure from Africa was lulled by the time he entered King Edward's Grammar School, a Tudor foundation salvaged from the wreck of the monasteries during the Reformation of the 1530's, to embark on scholarship, a genteel road to a living for a clever poor boy. His mother died in 1910, and the boy entered almost wholly the all too male world of private education. One guardian was Francis Xavier Morgan, a priest of the Birmingham Oratory, who, says Tolkien, was half Spanish. The Tolkiens by this time were Catholic converts, and Morgan was Tolkien's pilot, a sort of father-image. The old-fashioned respect Tolkien has for the Cloth and his pious and practicing Catholicism are his heritage from Oratorian Morgan.

The Birmingham Oratory was John Henry, Cardinal Newman's foundation and retreat. There, away from London, where his feline and impossible companion in conversion, Faber, had ensconced himself as Master of the London Oratory, Newman tried to impact a leaven of Anglicanism and religiosity and learning to the raw immigrant or distant Roman Catholicism of England.

Newman established a school in Birmingham where a flock of young Catholics were educated; Belloc was one of them. There is a pathetic account of the old, worn, defeated Newman wandering in and out of the chalky, dusty classrooms while his teachers and disciples paused for a while in their instruction and shared with him the realization that there was no place or welcome for them in the burly, red-necked Roman Church in England. Tolkien must have known through Father Morgan some of the dusty feeling of defeat that pervaded the place. It went through a period of decline so abysmal that even the other Catholic schools noticed it, but renovated and reformed it can never be better than the idea of the Public School, which was bad at the beginning and gets worse every year. Tolkien was to send his three sons to that Oratory school.

It was wise to send Tolkien to King Edward's School, where there was some tradition of scholarship, as a day boy; it led him to Oxford on a scholarship, and there he graduated from Exeter College in 1915.

He was twenty-three then and, like all of his generation

11

of Englishmen, young lions under the donkey, went to war. He was married, a love match, before he went to the Front, in 1916. There had been obstacles placed in the way of his marriage; his faith and poor prospects particularly were not the sort of attributes Edith Bratt's guardians were looking for. He was no plum in the marriage garden, but they married anyhow and have been together ever since.

Tolkien served in the sacrificial role of an infantry soldier in the Lancashire Fusiliers, one of the good county regiments that inevitably suffered great casualties. He, who set such store by and so needed friendship, had but one friend left when the war was over, and friends, for Tolkien as for all, are hard to come by and then to keep.

After service on the Western Front, in the trenches, around Bapaume, he was invalided back to Britain. He lay in a hospital bed and there, perhaps unconsciously, ordered his life, although he could not have known what this order would bring forth. Old soldiers deny that their experience has any real bearing on their future, but it does. Tolkien's war had an influence on him as strong as his childhood, although he may not know it and does deny it, for those who served in the trenches in World War I were never the same again. C.S. Lewis, whom Tolkien knew for many years, "a very busy official and teacher," as Tolkien dryly described him, and with whom he shared much of the reading of his subcreation, was a soldier too; Lewis has written that *The Lord of the Rings,* Tolkien's great work, reflects much of the experiences both of them endured in the war: the still and ominous quiet, the sudden comradeship, the surprise of joy in the most unexpected places. Lewis was never to forget it. He sought it all his life thereafter, as Tolkien never even thought of doing, being sufficient to himself and his own reflection.

England was never the same again after World War I, a catalysis. She was drained nearly to death. Some of the lowering background of danger of the imminent fall of Right, apprehension, hangs over all of *The Lord of the Rings*. Tolkien learned the language of it lying on his sickbed, and language has magic in it. A lord of language, Tolkien has broken through the crust of the alphabet, of the normal spelling, into the spelling of the supernatural.

Yet his spelling on first reading is simple and easy: there is his great skill.

Long before reading, if ever that even comes, that spelling is a skill still beyond the grasp of most of the world, the Being that issues from the womb. It cries out the same call over the world, turns to the Mother for succor, seeks a Father, begins to experience life, is conditioned from the very moment of birth and before by environment and the inimical forces that surround it. Under the most auspicious circumstances, as at the birth of a prince of legend, Being is surrounded by differences and barriers. This is the theme of many fairy stories and, Tolkien said in his Andrew Lang lecture in 1939, is the stuff of fairy stories. They are not meant for children. Indeed, bowdlerized in the mistaken idea that this makes them good for children—as if bowdlerizing were good for anything, let alone children—they have had their whole pith extracted, so children get stones when they expect good bread.

A stickly kind of sentimentality has produced "a dreadful undergrowth" of stories fashioned to provide what is considered to be suitable for children. The old stories are bowdlerized, and silly, false copies made of them, like those reproductions of paintings where women's breasts and bellies are flat, washed out. Even worse, fairy stories are often ruined for children, and children ruined too, by being told in a covert, shy and prurient way, with an eye cocked by the teller for the knowing approval of the grown-up. This is a demeaning of childhood, a sin that cries for vengeance. Humility and innocence, the very heart of a child, are necessary for any great adventure. When that heart is in the very body and mind of a child, it should be treated with reverence and respect, never lisped or babbled or talked over the head of. Tolkien quotes Chesterton: "For children are innocent and love justice while most of us are wicked, and naturally prefer mercy." There is more harm done to children by denying them the truth, by preferring appetites or self to them, than can ever be forgiven or redressed.

As a child, Tolkien did not particularly care for fairy stories. He says so in that Andrew Lang lecture that he delivered at St. Andrew's University in 1939. It was at

13

school, not a golden time for him but sad and troubled, that he came to fairy stories, and he liked other things as well or better—history, botany, grammar and the study of words. Poetry he came to love later by seeking the words to translate classical verse. "A real taste for fairy stories was wakened by philology on the threshold of manhood, and quickened to full life by the war." That is about as much as Tolkien will ever say about the beginning of his work, and it's enough.

The fact is, as Tolkien related in that troubled year of 1939, children are never meant to be Peter Pans; they are meant to grow up, not necessarily thereby losing their innocence and wonder but in danger of losing them on their appointed journey, in danger mainly from grown-ups, from people into whose charge they are delivered. This is an awful, inescapable fact. The journey is one that all must make, "that journey up which it is certainly not better to travel hopefully than to arrive, though we must travel hopefully if we are to arrive." A great lesson of fairy stories Tolkien carries into his work is that "on callow, lumpish and selfish youth peril, sorrow and the shadow of death can bestow dignity, and even sometimes wisdom."

He loathes fictional, pretty children, dressed up to look like garden elves; if there is a bloody fight, let there be one, with no excuses. His blue eyes sparkle at the thought of a good fight. "If fairy story as a kind is worth reading at all it is worthy to be written for and read by adults." Then, he says, children may hope to get fairy stories fit to read. Tolkien avers that it is always best for children to read a bit above their heads so that their books, like their clothes, will allow room to grow in. In any case, it is for their own peace of mind that grown-ups cling to the belief that children are simpler than they really are. *The Lord of the Flies, Catcher in the Rye, Huckleberry Finn* and *Kim* show how far off-base is this adult anodyne.

Helen MacMillan Buckhurst was an Oxford colleague of Tolkien, a godmother in his home. She was an Icelandic scholar, a lover of Norse myth. Professor Katherine Ball of Toronto University was a student of hers at Saint Hugh's during the twenties. Helen Buckhurst told her that Tolkien, on his hospital bed after the war, resolved to learn Language and the roots of it as his life's work, and he did. Tolkien was a born teacher, too. Out of his healing time Tolkien came, ready to grow in his field.

Language is to many the ability to order a meal in Paris, to say Racine so that it sounds like a French author and not a town in Wisconsin, to escape the exploitation of the hick in Rome, to do business in Sweden, to expound on the communist literary canon with feeling, to don academic profundity, to be a pundit, to claim to understand what Schnitzler really said. Language is regarded by most at its very best as a means to an end, and philologists use the language ploy to keep students in thrall, use academic politics and skulduggery lest their courses be knocked out of the college curriculum and replaced with the language of business administration, the thesaurus of computer science. Language, to Tolkien, is a means in itself. Deep within it is a cry for help, for love, and behind it is the whole of the human condition that becomes more and more tangled and hidden as the world turns and grows in man. There is more Language in an infant's cry, a yell or a laugh than man can tell in words.

It was 1919 before Tolkien got to scholarship again. Then for two years he worked as an assistant on the *Oxford English Dictionary*, one of the great books of the tongue. Five million and more excerpts were collected and nearly two million were selected to show the usage of the English word. The word is traced to its beginning, framed in use, the use changing with the times. Tolkien assisted in the revision of that enterprise, lived with words, assembled them, framed them in context. It was this work with words that in the end made him a collaborator, in the 1960's, in the translation of the Jerusalem Bible from the French. He did Job; he would have done Judges better. A work of scholarship and lore, scholars, critics and divines hail it as a landmark in Bible making, even if the King James still rules the Englished Word.

Then, with his family growing, he started his life of university teaching, at the University of Leeds as Reader in the English Language in 1921. Within four years he became Professor. A Professor is more important in England than in America. There is generally only one in a department, the Chairman, and the position carries weight and prestige. Tolkien came to this post young, just entering his thirties.

Tolkien received the call to Oxford almost immediately after he became Professor at Leeds. There for twenty years, until the end of World War II, he was Rawlinson Professor of Anglo-Saxon and Fellow of Pembroke College. Then he became Merton Professor of English Literature and lived in a College house on Holywell, which descended to his son Christopher on his retirement, as did also some of his teaching.

The Fellows of the Oxford colleges live in a male, closed society, surrounded by ancient or mock-ancient walls, a compact group bound together whether they like it or not (it can be hell for the wives, and generally is). Chosen young students come to them for a unique and inimitable system of education, now threatened by the growth of the graduate schools. The Fellows often live in if they are unmarried or free, and all have rooms in the College where they meet their students in constant tutorial encounter. They dine together often and collogue, scheme and make their ploys in the Senior Common Room, gossip, make mischief or regale one another with their own company.

It is a closed community with the virtues and the vices, most of all the vice of *accidie*, of that order. It carries with it advantages, the chance of male companionship perhaps above all. That can be the most desired and hardest to find of some men's needs once they grow up. It is not growing up, but a defense against it, against the enemy of Time. It is the answer, the only one, to some men's loneliness. It is a terrible thing to have no friends to help or to summon to one's aid. This is the great vrtue of the Family, where, as Robert Frost said, "they have to take you in."

Tolkien flowered in the Oxford of his days, as he had grown there in his youth. To a man such as he, with the sorrow of his childhood, life there, even wedded and with a family, was good. While at Leeds he had already published *A Middle English Vocabulary* and his famous edition of *Sir Gawaine and the Green Knight* with E. V. Gordon, which had made his name known in the classrooms.

But it was his address before the British Association in

16

1936, "*Beowulf*: The Monsters and the Critics," that made his mark. It makes good reading, strong and vigorous against those whose neglect the poetry of the saga, of literature, in their picking and prying, raising "the dust of the quarrying researchers." He comes to the aid of dragons, shows them as real as truth. Scholarship and piety mixed with the poetic realization of a subcreator make this address the landmark of learning in the field it has become and make of Tolkien a contradictory and bewildering man to get hold of in print. "Tolkien and I were talking of dragons," said C.S. Lewis once, as naturally as if they had been talking about the weather. Dragons were as everyday and real as the weather to them, far more fearsome than any mortal storm, was the intention of his anecdote.

Tolkien's lectures at Oxford became popular beyond all normal bounds for philology. Michael Innes, the pen name of the Oxford don and detective story writer J.M. Stewart, says that during Tolkien's lectures it seemed as if the woods and nature had come into the dusty hall with a rustle of leaves. A Professor at the Graduate School of the University of Toronto remembers Tolkien lecturing in 1926 and says,

He came in lightly and gracefully, I always remember that, his gown flowing, his fair hair shining, and he read *Beowulf* aloud. We did not know the language he was reading, yet the sound of Tolkien made sense of the unknown tongue and the terrors and the dangers that he recounted—how I do not know—made our hair stand on end. He read like no one else I have ever heard. The lecture room was crowded—it was in the Examination Halls, and he was a young man then, for his position, long before *The Hobbit* or the Trilogy were to make him famous. I took a seminar from him also, on Gothic. He was a great teacher, and delightful, courteous, ever so kindly.

Another student said:

He had his faults. He would ruffle through his notes rapidly, speaking in a quick, almost stuttering monotone until he struck something that interested him. Then he would light up, expand, expound. He took endless pains with his students, helped them so much that work they published—he published very little himself—was really his own. Yet he never took credit for this, only pleasure for his pupils. He was a great teacher, and you are lucky if you encounter even one in your whole learning lark.

Tolkien gave the Andrew Lang lecture on the Fairy Story at Saint Andrew's University in 1939 and set the record straight again: fairy stories were not intended for children. This essay, included in the Ballantine paperback *The Tolkien Reader,* is easy reading, for a scholarly essay, and makes a good preface to *The Lord of the Rings*.

He gave the W.P. Ker lecture at Glasgow University in 1933, and he holds honorary degrees from University College, Dublin, and the University of Liège. These degrees were given for his scholarship, not for his fantasy or any official hole that he might fall into. The W.P. Ker lecture at Glasgow is given to scholars and students of that university; Common Sense is Glasgow, and Tolkien is a no-nonsense man, perhaps too much so. His dragons, trolls and Ringwraiths are all too terribly real, and he is the first to admit it.

But for the illness of his wife he was to have come to America in 1957 to accept honorary degrees from Marquette, Harvard and several other universities and to deliver a series of addresses. That was not to be; he never came, has never left Britain since he arrived there in his childhood, save for the odd trip to Europe. His fame in America is a puzzle to him, although it pleases, perplexes and bothers him. It's a tangent from his real purpose as a writer, a by-product that bewilders not only himself but others and has brought with it a plethora of mail he finds it difficult to cope with. He has no idea how to delegate fan mail, or anything else.

He wrote *The Hobbit* in the thirties for his children; it was published in England in 1938 with his own illustrations. This edition was ruined in the blitz. In the beginning he wrote it, it seems, to read aloud to his children. This, he thinks, has weakened it; but he did please them.

He is above all a fond father. He has a lovely script, and it was written on all sorts of paper: exercise books, scraps, ruled foolscap and the like. It was read for a while to other Oxford people in manuscript until it was, to his pleasure and surprise, regarded as a piece of publishable material. Since then it has gone from impression to impression, a steady, unspectacular seller, and from language to language; it is the precursor of *The Lord of the Rings*. The illustrations vary from country to country and show the varying interpretations of the Hobbits. Gradually Tolkien's own illustrations are being accepted as the best, but it has taken time for this to be realized.

All too often Tolkien has been read as if he were someone else, such as C.S. Lewis. Yet an appreciation of C.S. Lewis is essential for those who would read Tolkien, not because the two men are similar, as they seem to be on the surface, but because they are not. Lewis was a famous don, the most famous, outside Oxford, of his generation. A son of Ulster, he was a brilliant expositor, a radio personality, a good scholar—his *Allegory of Love* may be a classic—a tutor who left his mark on many students, a profoundly troubled and perplexed man who found a haven in Christianity. He gathered around him for spiritual comfort all he could. For years his life and actions and beliefs grew around Tolkien's. Tolkien has been tarred by his brush. That has led to a misunderstanding of Tolkien and his work that is worse than any denunciation of it. To make a Lewis of Tolkien is like making a jolly green giant out of Gargantua.

CHAPTER II

THE INKLINGS AND THE MYTH

The Inklings were a group that met more or less regularly on Thursday nights in Lewis' rooms at Magdalen College, or elsewhere, in "The Lamb and Flag," "The Eagle and Child," "The Burning Babe" and other pubs, generally in the small private saloon bars, a feature of old taverns. "A famous and heroic gathering, one that has already passed into literary legend."

W.H. Lewis was often there. A close companion and more of his brother Clive, he had troubles of his own, his cross to bear, like all men. He has described the meetings of the Inklings with gusto and affectionate recollection. It almost sounds like a gathering of unusually literate Hobbits. Take, for example, this meeting in Lewis' Magdalen College rooms:

> When half a dozen or so had arrived, tea would be produced, and then when pipes were well alight Jack [C.S. Lewis] would say, "Well, has nobody got anything to read us?"*

Somehow this brief quotation catches all the jolly goodness, the contrived, desired and sought-for simplicity that Lewis hugged like a Dutch wife, and wherein the others also relaxed themselves.

Then the manuscripts would be pulled out of pockets or wallets, and after the reading would come the judgment that was never prissy but sound and frank, and brutal if need be. W.H. Lewis recalls that 1946 was a vintage year for the Inklings. "At most of the meetings during that year we had a chapter from Tolkien's 'new Hobbit' as we called it—the great work later published as *The Lord of the Rings*." For years they heard bits of the new Hobbit book, and some were frank enough to groan aloud when more of it came from Tolkien's pockets. Later, because of Tolkien's attitude to criticism, they had his son Christopher, from New College read it to them, but nothing they said ever influenced the maker of *The Rings*. He was as impervious to criticism as he was, deep down, impervious to Everyman, and remains so.

The criticisms directed at this book by the Inklings and the influence some wishful thinkers would like to claim were of no account whatever. Replying to Charles Moorman, who was contemplating a book upon the influence

---

* W.H. Lewis, ed., *Letters of C.S. Lewis* (New York: Harcourt, Brace and World, 1966), p. 13.

this group had upon one another—and what a book!—Lewis replied, "No one ever influenced Tolkien—you might as well try to influence a bandersnatch."* They listened to Tolkien's reading and later to Christopher's, but only their encouragement pleased him. "He has only two reactions to criticism; either he begins the whole thing over again from the beginning or else takes no notice at all." Listening to Tolkien, looking at him bubbling with his inner humor as he expostulated like a Victorian, experiencing his old-fashioned good manners, sharing most of his formal creed of conduct and behavior, the Inklings experienced a rather wan sensation of non-rapport, such as one might get talking to Roy Campbell about colonial novelists or effete poets.

Lewis denies in another letter that there was any sort of allegory in *The Lord of the Rings*: the Ring was no symbol of the mushroom ring of destruction that accompanies a nuclear bomb. Allegory in any case was a dirty word to Tolkien, as it was not to Lewis, whose only first-class book is his *Allegory of Love*. Lewis pointed out in his letter that Tolkien began his Romance before the bomb was invented, but this is of no more account than the assertion that Icarus flew before satellites were blasted.

Christopher Tolkien, J.R.R.'s second son, was with the Royal Air Force in South Africa when *The Lord of the Rings* was in early process of subcreation, and although his father sent him drafts to read, he is sure that no comments of his made the slightest difference. The Trilogy took Tolkien years to write, for he had promises to keep, a war to live through and his teaching. And his nature must have warred against the vast ordered task of it, for, as C.S. Lewis says of him, he is "a great but dilatory and unmethodical man." This need not be true, but there is a lot in it, more than meets the eye.

Lewis was prompted to that remark by a lady's question about a book that he was somehow scheduled to do in collaboration with Tolkien. That book, he said, was dated, he feared, to appear on the Greek Calends, and he was right. Save for scholarly collaboration, as in his edition with Gordon of *Sir Gawaine and the Green Knight,* or in en-

* *Ibid.*, p. 287.

21

couraging, even rewriting, his students' work, Tolkien was no man's partner.

The amount of work these men got through was remarkable. C.S. Lewis published far too much, Tolkien too little. All the while they found time to relish or share in one another's company—they would have been at a loss without it—to write a lot of letters, generally in longhand, to seekers and friends, to conduct their academic business and to teach. The ripest are often kindest to the rawest, and they were all good to others and for themselves. There are students everywhere of their days, dons now, most of them, writers, mind movers some, who testify to the constant attention, the frequent kindness that they received from the hands of these masters. Christopher Tolkien retains a most affectionate memory of Lewis. John Leyerle, Director of the Centre for Medieval Studies at the University of Toronto, a pupil of Tolkien, says that nothing was ever too much trouble for Tolkien to take over him when he was at Oxford, that for ever after there was a bond between the teacher and the taught that went far beyond the normal obligation; many others have told that, in varying degrees. However much the students gave, they got back in spades, were shown where to dig and often found the ground planted for them.

There was more to this jolly company, Inklings and all, than appears at first reading from their own memories. On the night that they had dinner at the "Eastgate," as Lewis recalls jovially, after the "roaring cataract of nonsense" that Dyson contributed, there was a reading of an original Christmas play by Charles Williams, a chapter of *The Lord of the Rings* by Tolkien and some of *The Problem of Pain* by Lewis himself.

Hugo Dyson was a newcomer to the Inklings, a seventeenth century scholar, "a most fastidious bookman . . . but as far from being a dilettante as anyone can be; a burly man, both in mind and body, with the stamp of war on him. . . . He is a Christian and a lover of cats."* The description is downright embarrassing, and yet so Lewis wrote, and it was as true in parts as a curate's egg. And to

* *Ibid.*, p. 145.

all Englishmen who were raised in their youth on the schoolboy exuberance of Frank Richards, creator of the remove form at Greyfriars School, there is more than a touch of the ink-stained Eton collar about it all.

Frank Richards-type school stories had a great effect on young England, affecting even the speech patterns of those boys, now grown into seeming men, who never went away to Public Schools but tried to believe they nearly did and were encouraged to do so. Even if their school was Cardiff Higher Grade, there were shades of Eton, of Lampeter anyhow, about the place, and there still are, state-supported though these schools are. It is all rather sad and silly. Thus Tolkien's Hobbits speak this Frank Richards, Harry Wharton English most of the time, and it must bewilder Americans and raise a chuckle among fewer and fewer Englishmen, yet Hobbits could speak no other way and still be Tolkien.

These school stories abounded in England, as nowhere else in the world. It all started in the mid-nineteenth century when Public Schools, so called because they originally were free and public, not private and privileged, emerged as boarding schools to raise a privileged and ruling class. Boys were sent away from home to them, pulled away from their families all too young. They learned there to speak a Public School English that branded the rest of the population on the tongue for not speaking as they did. The schools were odd, brutal, stark academics of conformity and muscular Christianity. The boys and masters were to a large extent divorced from the care and the company of women, so homosexuality tended to be rife or suspected. There was bullying. They were a vile creation and remain so, an anomaly in this age or in any other.

There have been many novels about them, from the silly and saccharine *Mr. Chips* to the *Stalky and Co.* stories of Kipling. But every week, for at least two generations until the war began in 1939, twopenny full-length novels about Public School life were issued, all seemingly written by one man, Frank Richards, in which a Public School fictional image, even tongue, was created, causing all the reading boys of England, and their sisters, to affect it. Most of the readers never even saw a Public School, but

23

all copied it in their ways, and as grown-ups they still do, implicitly by their pathetic simulation embracing the rod of the caste system that is England's bane.

Tolkien did not go to a Public School, as poor Lewis did, yet the Inklings were men of a kind. They were generally traditional believers, though as Lewis was warned in the English Faculty at Oxford, both implicitly and explicitly, Tolkien was also a papist and a philologist, two things to be leery of in any man, especially when they come together. Yet there was an affinity among these men; they relished their own company; they shared a common ground and round, their daily work; and, as is evident, there was no nonsense about leaning on one another for help about plumbing, salary or family affairs. They were a self-indulgent group, encouraged by the Oxford climate to climb, tangle and luxiuriate, grow rank even.

Nevil Coghill, the Chaucer scholar, was another of the Inklings, and Coghill brought Charles Williams into the circle. Williams, manager of the Oxford Press, came to Oxford when the Press moved there from Amen Square in London during the war.

Williams fascinated Lewis, above all, who used his friends almost like ice floes in a dark and deep stream, his life, that he had to cross. And Lewis, who seemed to be the scape of his own goat since childhood, leaped from Tolkien to Williams. Books streamed from Williams' pen; his lectures were spell-binders. His novels—*Descent into Hell* is the best—are favorites of seekers after thrills and grace. Largely self-educated, he had a vivid Celtic wealth of imagery, which Hugo Dyson called "clotted glory." The other Inklings liked him in degrees, according to their needs and natures. He was vulgar in diction and wide-open to barbs in academic society.

"But he is a lovely creature. I'm proud of being among his friends," Tolkien grinned a little—he has quite a grin—and accepted Williams far more equally and on his own terms.

Charles Williams came from the lower middle class, with a high school education and a Cockney accent that branded him on the tongue in that Oxford society. Yet men such as Gervase Mathew, Tolkien and Dyson shared

24

Lewis' affection for him, although not so wildly his enthusiasm. And, along with Lewis and Tolkien, he became the best known of the Inklings. Certainly, Tolkien and Williams, with Dyson, were the main men who drew Lewis along his way, as Dyson and Tolkien, Lewis says, had first started him on it. Williams must have been an endearing man. His accent ceased to grate when he started to hold forth. His face would become quite ecstatic in his enthusiasm. "In public and in private he is of nearly all the men I have met, the one whose address most overflows with *love*,"* said Lewis about him; about the Inklings Lewis said:

> Williams, Dyson of Reading and my brother (Anglicans) and Tolkien and Havard (our doctor), your Church [Catholic], are the "Inklings" to whom my *Problem of Pain* was dedicated. We meet on Friday evenings in my rooms. . . . What I owe to them all is incalcuable. . . . Is any pleasure on earth as great as a circle of Christian friends by a good fire?**

There is that Frank Richards language and feeling dripping out of Lewis again.

Several writers, Professor M.E. Wright in her *Cosmic Kingdom of Myth*, Dr. Robert Reilly in his *Romantic Religion in the Work of Owen Barfield, C.S. Lewis, Charles Williams and J.R.R. Tolkien*, Margaret Grennan, Charles Moorman, Chad Walsh and Alice Hadfield—the number increases almost by the month, the academic mills are working overtime on the "Oxford Christians," as one writer has wretchedly designated them—point out that Lewis sometimes seems to echo Tolkien, and in the three men, Lewis, Williams and Tolkien, similarities of thought and interest have been explored frequently and at length. These pundits are all wrong, they multiply the error that is deep-rooted and mischievous. Of course the three of them share the theme of "there and back again" that is intrinsic to *The Hobbit* and is the winding and the binding of

* *Ibid.*, p. 196.
** *Ibid.*, p. 197.

The Lord of the Rings. But the critics fail to see that the differences between these men are far more important than the appearance of their likenesses.

Hegel, of course, plays a part in the critics' talk about the There and Back Again syndrome. One critic, W.R. Irwin, even quotes him:

> Inherent in the strange and remote is a powerful interest . . . the attractiveness of which is in inverse proportion to its familiarity. . . . Initially it is in that remoteness that depth must be sought; this is a necessary seeking for illusion. But the depth and strength which we attain can be measured only by the distance to which we have fled from the familiar centre where we first found ourselves embedded, and to which we strive to return.

This distance, retaining strands that lead us back again, relieves the writer of the onus of the present and sets him free to soar, to observe from a distance and apart action and resolution that have a bearing on his own condition yet can only be observed in another dimension. This is the achievement of Fantasy, or Romance, which is, as the *Oxford English Dictionary* has it, "a fictitious narrative in prose of which the scene and incidents are very remote from those of ordinary life." This is what the so-called trio (Williams, Lewis and Tolkien) set out to achieve, all independently, however, and with different results: Williams best with his *Descent into Hell*, Lewis with his *Perelendra* and other seemingly science-fiction stories and Tolkien with his *Lord of the Rings*. Tolkien was successful; the other two failed. Trio they were not, never were.

In Tolkien there is always present a grave, nigh-unto-death encounter with the forces of Evil, and invariably, after great hazard and suffering, even to the end, there is not so much a victory won, as time, time gained by the Right Order to recover from the loss and be more or less prepared for the next inevitable but unforeseen affray. Gandalf the wizard is ever the voice of his concern. Always Evil is feared and the strength of it realized; there is never any suggestion that Right will triumph just by being right, though in the school stories a small boy was often gulled

26

into challenging the bad bully because he was bad. In reality, of course, the good little boy gets beaten up as a result, for not only are bullies wrong and repulsive, but they are usually roustabouts and hard-fisted, crafty, dirty fighters, too.

Tolkien heroes never despair; they know that although the night will be a smothering blanket of dark and the floods of Evil will lap against the very brim of their protection, even break through here and there and devastate, the dawn will come, has come so far already, the dark is getting paler all the time, the walls will hold, the waters will ebb. Thus Tolkien relates his art with his belief, his formal Christian doctrine, wholly successfully, yet with never a Holy Name. With the other two, Lewis and Williams, propaganda, the antithesis of Art, shows through. And while all Art is propaganda, the slightest sign of it in the creative or subcreative work is a blemish that can curdle and ruin, as it will ruin the work of Williams and Lewis in another generation. Artists deny their propaganda and believe themselves. But their work is all the stronger for being objective.

The three of them accept the traditional pattern of romantic fiction, of a Quest, a journey fraught with hazards, even horror, and a safe return; this is classic. Man is never alone in those enterprises whereby his heroic efforts save his, his God's, world. Prester John and Simon Magus appear to help in the novels of Williams, the hross and sorns are among the extra-human agents who give aid to Lewis' man Ransom, along with Merlin, the bear Bultitude and the Fisher King. Tolkein's Orcs, Trolls, wizards, Ents, dwarves and Ringwraiths are other than human too, but they are realizable to the reader. They dwell in the past of his mind, and it needs only the magic of Romance to bring them alive again. These books have been called "spiritual thrillers," but the title belittles them: they are much better than that. Indeed, they have something in common with *The Pyx* by J. Buell, *A Hint of an Explanation* by Graham Greene and *Tremor of Intent* by Anthony Burgess.

Not only are there prodigious happenings in all their fantastic stories, but Man is involved in them all, often reluctantly, but always by his own will. It is only in the subcreation of the Hobbit, by not making a man of the Hobbit, that Tolkien realizes and brings home the significance of Man's participation, the lonely and peculiar estate of Man in the Universe. The damned and ultimate losers, so far, are those who seek, grasp and use Power for their own ends against the Order of Things, while those who release themselves from all that is dear in order to follow Right obtain a victory, however fleeting and transient, a state of holy renown and a memory of their good deeds in men's minds and stories. Tolkien's sub-creation is not as clear-cut as all this; he has a tendency to ramble and to be finicky, but he is the best of all who have essayed this in the vernacular of these days. The message is there for those who can read it.

The language and the power of it are of the utmost importance in his works. Charles Williams has a spouting of imagery and imagination; he is possessed of the *hwyl*, a benevolent Celtic form of possession similar to the apocalyptic gift of tongues, as he calls up his heroes from the past and indulges both himself and the reader in the language of the Christian liturgy and prayer. Thus in *War in Heaven* Williams shows his skill by omitting rather than committing language. When Prester John, who comes to earth to help Man in battle against those who are leagued with the Devil, approaches the altar, priest-king to celebrate Mass in the old English Church, the Duke of the North Ridings follows the liturgy beginning at the *Introibo* rather sleepily, as cradle-Catholics do, but wakes up with a start when he realizes that Prester John has omitted the *Confiteor,* for he is God and does not confess. Again at the Consecration there is a break in the liturgy of the Mass, for God is the celebrant. It is effective, this use of language by omission, it speaks louder than words.

Lewis, who began by suspecting both Christians and philologists and many other things after his wretched father-relation and school, makes his hero, Ransom, a philologist and a Christian. The language known as Old Solar is the tongue common among the inhabitants of Mars in this trilogy of Fantasy, and Ransom learns it; it becomes his tongue in *Perelandra,* although perforce he used Latin to converse with Merlin Ambrosius.

The power of language is invoked again in *That*

Hideous Strength, in which the devils behind the National Institute of Coordinated Research twist the English language to their own purposes and befoul it into improper use to promote misunderstanding in the way that George Orwell's leaders do in their perversion, Newspeak, in *1984*. The Father of Lies is one of Beelzebub's titles, and it is by the use of language, nothing else, as Lewis illustrates, that Hell can almost take over. There is an ugly atavism in Lewis' account of their defeat, as if, when prayer fails, recourse to violence is justified.

Tolkien makes all previous use of language sound pale in his subcreation. He wields it as easily as a backwoodsman handles his rifle. His works are couched in the traditional language and parlance of the heroic and courtly tale, when this is proper. The Hobbits' speech is down-to-earth; they speak merrily whenever possible, with words and echoes of words that are common to young larking lads or as easy and as comfortable and as wheezing as old shoes. This must be borne; Tolkien could not have done otherwise. All that jars in *The Lord of the Rings* jars because Tolkien, none other, wrote it, and there could have been no such great work otherwise.

There are riddle and slogan, curses couched in the formal pattern of malediction, evocations and incantations, songs of all kinds, rhymes, verses and poetry, the brave talk that keeps the courage up and the slippery talk that leads to treachery. Tolkien keeps the reader fully aware, if too abundantly, personally and eruditely, of the language as it fitted for him the time, place and pattern of the story. Westron, the tongue of the Dúnedain, is the common tongue, but there is Elvish—Tolkien says, bewilderingly, that this should be his language for writing *The Lord of the Rings*—and there are the ancient tongues of Eldarin. The Elvish of Tolkien is his peculiar thing. He has composed the Elvish rubric and can sing it well and eerily, in a sort of Gregorian chant. And it makes sense; there's the magic of it. It is better to hear, and more moving, than most of the Latin rubric that hardly anyone understands or listens to outside the choir stalls of a monastery, maybe.

Then there are Dwarvish and Orkish. The Ents, the trees that move, have, very understandably, a language of their own. Runic writing abounds and is a source of power, for therein are couched great incantations and wisdom of the past that Gandalf the white wizard can control by his learning.

Somehow, for all this, the reader has to know of it, for Tolkien keeps the language of his tale in Westron, the language of the West. He writes in English, and it would be well if he left it at that and published the appendixes, indexes, and prefaces apart. The whole theme of his work does not depend upon the evolving or the involving of characters. The theme of his tale is subtly dialectical and needs to be so to succeed. He goes beyond the present clamant and individual dilemma to an everlasting and cosmic situation, further than he knows or cares to. He has created a body of lore that is beyond his control, a living thing.

In every case, however, to return to the unrelated trio, they manage characters that relate to their own aspirations, questions and needs. They accomplish this each in his own way. Williams creates characters that step out of a cocktail party in Westchester on All Hallows Eve and involve themselves, much to their surprise. Lewis makes his people out of the world around him, the rather smug little higgledypiggledy world that he had made for himself and where he welcomed his friends and wrestled with and tried to solve his own besetting, ever grave problems and afflictions.

Tolkien projected his Hobbits to establish this relation, and he does it successfully, being a whole man, unlike Lewis or Williams. The Hobbits seem to belong to the natural order, though they are beyond the ken and vision of all men, for Tolkien persuades us that they may be around as surely as an exaltation of larks or a slink of foxes. Tolkien so completely realizes them in his imagination that he shares with them not only in their pleasure, such as laughter and good company before the fire, which most proper men relish, but in their preoccupation with their family trees and in a dismay and dislike for the pretensions of their kin, such as the Sackville-Bagginses, although, truth to tell, perhaps it was too much Took blood in Bilbo that started all the troubles that came with his return with that dratted Ring. The Hobbits are as silly and as preoccupied with family trees as Tolkien is, or the Welsh are. As if there always was something wild about the Took family of Hobbits, Belladonna Took became a Baggins, Bilbo's wife, and there was some talk of fairy blood in her that may have started the whole thing, the matter of the Rings. It's all in the blood, they seem to say, and the silly boobies may be right.

Somehow Man is freed by his Hobbit relation. Free of his body's frame and situation, he can share in those that are of Cosmic Kind. The Hobbit remains familiar to the reader while bringing him into the very essence of being. The scientists maintain that it is almost impossible to conceive that there is no life other than that Man knows and owns. This scientific hypothesis is shown by Tolkien as truer than Truth. It is hard not to believe him, better to. If man only trusts his senses, he has no idea of what is going on around him and within him.

There is one thing shared by all mankind: myth, the precursor and necessary ingredient in all the writings of Tolkien, an essential part of his realtion. Myth is the stripping and polishing into the memory of the race their memorable past and people. Every society has it to a degree; it is built into the computer of the brain as an essential addition to whatever conclusions are reached. As much a part of Man as his skin and bone, it affects all his thought, and he often knows it not. James Kennaway, in *Tunes of Glory*, catches something of what myth can do, even to a bagpipe tune, when the listener is Gaelic and the air is a pibroch:

To the unpractised ear a pibroch has no form or melody, and to the accustomed ear it has little more. But it is a mood, and a pibroch was something that Jock felt almost physically; damp penetrating and sad like a mist.

Myth is more than a memory: it is physically imbued from the earth and the air of the folk. Myth becomes vulgarized and forgotten when once a folk moves from the place of its ancient dwelling, so that within a generation the myth of the race no longer has a hold, a bond or a relation, save in the case of the Jews. Witness the Irish in America, the English in the Antipodes, the Sicilians in

Lombardy; all is changed, and new roots have to be established. That takes time, and the new myth is vulgar. So it is especially among long-rooted people, among the British, for example, that the myth strongly prevails upon their minds and actions. Tolkien uses his art to the full to relate it to this time with his Hobbits.

Yet the myth of Britain goes far beyond the Island, as Owen Barfield, scholar and a sometime Inkling, shows in his books. Save for the Graeco-Roman occupation experience, missed largely by most of Britain, the myth of the Islands is largely Norse and Teutonic, Celtic and perhaps Syrian—from the Phoenician traders and the Nestorians perhaps, from the learning that came from Byzantium through the Middle Ages, along with all the syncretic pattern surrounding the gospels and the lives of Christians. Here Hebraic myth, legend and learning also enter in, and Sanskrit too.

The learning of Tolkien, his background and rearing, does affect his use of myth and imbue it, because of the man he is, with a kind of jolly boyish innocence that comes strangely to readers unaware of the man, his life, social milieu and education. Once, in *Till We Have Faces,* Lewis interpreted anew the classical myth of Psyche and Cupid, but this is by no means his best work in the field of Romance and was written for the times, the fifties, almost as if to show he was not bound by his past, as all men are, but lived in the current psychological swim. *Phantastes,* by George MacDonald, *Islandia,* by Wright, Eddison's *The Worm Ouroboros* are all precursors in the use of myth. Ulsterman Lewis praises George MacDonald, his master, he claimed, far too much, and the whole thrust and pattern of Tolkien were far beyond what had gone before.

CHAPTER III

THE DAYS OF THE DONS

Artists are didactic, but for the mind they seek to move this must not show, for it makes their work suspect, and properly so. One of the great things in favor of Tolkien, in the opinion of many of his readers who have rejected formal religion, and they are in the millions, is that there is no religion in *The Lord of the Rings*, though, in fact, it is all Religion. The story can be read for pleasure and the book closed; what happens after is within the reader. Some may enjoy the message without understanding, as some enjoy Beethoven for the fine noise.

Existing myth is not enough for Tolkien, any more than it was for Lewis or Williams. All three extend it far beyond the forms wherein they found it and create a new pattern on the old, fanning the lambent ember of myth that is deep in all into flame. Essentially myth is pre-literary; it tends to submerge into the unconscious with the proliferation of print; it belongs to an earlier form of the Word. There is some godliness in myth, as in all primitive recall, something as apocalyptic as the parted tongues of fire that hovered over every disciple in that upper room on the first Pentecost. A god walks and works in all of myth.

Lewis reveals this awareness, common to all myth, in his essay *On Stories:*

> To be stories at all they must be a series of events: but it must be understood that this series—the *plot* as we call it—is only really a net whereby to catch something else. The real theme may be, and perhaps usually is, something that has no sequence in it, but something

33

other than a process and much more like a state or quality.*

Myth becomes more and more elusive, shrouded in the thought and language of another age.

There is one real purpose in Story: to reveal a truth by a tale, a tale that can be read for itself with enjoyment and yet where, upon reflection—which may or may not come—Truth enters in, often as unwelcome and forbidding as a creed. Writers such as John Updike, William Faulkner, John O'Hara, Mary McCarthy, Edna O'Brien are sterner moralists than those who read them for reasons other than to uncover their morality—and that is nearly all—realize, and then the insight is only gained indirectly. Remarkably successful movies such as *Georgy Girl, Saturday Night and Sunday Morning, Alfie,* and *La Dolce Vita* owe their popularity to the direction and acting that embellish them and, more apparently than with the books, to the urgent desire to relate with the stern message that is so cleverly and frivolously presented; the crowd gets the message, even if it shrugs it off and continues its Gadarene Progress, which has always been Highway to Man.

There is an abiding contribution of Tolkien's own learning, reflection and background in his own work, yet unlike the contributions of both Lewis and Williams, and of other members of that Inkling group, it does not show through. This is what makes him a great writer, as the others are not. This is Art. He is extremely reticent about his life as it relates to his art, and here Tolkien is so unlike other writers of these days. But through his reticence may be quite admirable, it is exasperating, for his work and his life are all woven together.

February 2, 1967: I have been away for a short time owing to my wife's ill health and my own weariness. I have far too much to do. I dislike being written about, and the results to date have caused me both irritation and distaste. I vetoed being treated in one of the series *Contemporary Writers in Christian*

---

* D. Sayers, ed., *Essays Presented to Charles Williams* (New York: Oxford University Press, 1947).

Perspective published by Eerdmans. I will not attempt to do the same in regard to your project. But I hope you will make it literary (and as critical of that aspect as you like) and not personal. I have no inclination, in fact must refuse, to provide information about myself, family and family origin. In any case this would be a matter of considerable labour if it was to be any more use than the sufficient facts found in the English *Who's Who?*

Yet all through his work Tolkien is very much aware of the present as it relates to the past, and his own past so affects his work that it has fashioned and strengthened it, as well as diminished its literary significance. But this is beyond recourse. His fond indulgent love for the Hobbits excuses their silly delight in treating their own genealogy with respect and great interest, neglecting all else of the past as of little moment and concern. No matter how far away, into distant lands and time, Tolkien takes his characters—and the reader—there is always a feeling of Present-earth, as against the Middle-earth of his narrative encounter; there is always a feeling of this Age lighting up the past of the Great Years of the Third Age. He creates a valhalla of a sort, a Fiddler's Green where Frodo, battered, worn to death, finds haven with the heroes of the past. There is a certainty that, while there is a Great Year of Plenty and a hard-won peace on Middle-earth, the indolence of the Hobbits will again be interrupted. They will, the reader knows, again march with another company around Man to save him from the damnation of his own near-choosing, until perhaps there will be a final march, a total defeat.

All the time Tolkien toils over his great subcreation, which remains yet unfinished and probably never will be finished. He adds to it whenever he finds the time. It is with *The Silmarillion* and the legends that surround his work that he is currently subcreating when he can find the time that grows rarer and more fleeting with the years. His son, Christopher, who teaches in his place at Oxford and is so like his father in some ways, so fractious and unlike him in others, replied to some questions about Tolkien's present works.

Christopher explained the origin of the Tolkien name, a puzzle to many people—Cornish perhaps? It might well have been from the sound of it, but no:

March 1, 1967: The name is German in origin, a compound of "toll" meaning "mad" (cognate with English "dull") and kühn "brave" (=English "keen"), and so meaning "foolhardy". I believe there is an English surname "Rashbold". But my ancestor of that name came to England from Saxony in the 18th Century, and I am neither German, nor foolhardy—at any rate, not very. . . .

My eldest brother John is a secular priest. He has just become the parish priest of the city church in Stoke-on-Trent; before that he was for a long time the chaplain of Keele University in Staffordshire, as well as running a local parish. He is about 50.

My second brother, Michael, is married, and having for a long time been a school master at the Benedictine School, Ampleforth, has now gone over to the Jesuits and teaches at Stonyhurst in Lancashire. He has three children; the eldest is now doing an advanced degree at Oxford.

My sister Priscilla is a lecturer at a technical college.

I was in the R.A.F. during the war, a pilot, and spent 18 months in South Africa learning to fly (1944-45). After V.E. Day I was threatened with becoming a Physical Training Equipment Officer so I joined the Naval Air Arm. My father used to send me parts of *The Lord of the Rings* to read while I was in South Africa (simply because I read it as it was written, and so he sent it to me while I was away). I don't think a very great deal can have been sent this way, but it's over 20 years ago, and I don't remember very clearly. I very much doubt I had any critical effect upon it whatsoever. . . .

As early as 1957 Tolkien was engaged in the completion of *The Silmarillion* and other legends concerning *The Lord of the Rings*, a task that has engaged him for more than a decade, as fame, popularity, copyright problems, and troubles that come with growing old perplex, weary and concern him, and yet please him and keep his youth intact within him, where it has ever been——hidden but still there.

At one time it looked very likely that he would come to America, where his academic reputation, established by his scholarly work and borne witness to by scores of his former pupils now teaching in universities throughout America, has flourished suddenly, along with a common popularity with too much fad in it since the publication of *The Lord of the Rings* in 1956. But he wrote on Whit Sunday, 1957, in response to an invitation from an American university to receive an honorary degree and deliver a series of lectures:

I have ill repaid the generosity of Marquette by my discourtesy of silence. Without going into long details this has been due not to lack of pleasure, (indeed excitement and delight) in the generous invitation, but to overwork, difficult domestic and academic circumstances, and the necessity of coping (or trying to cope) with a now very large mail, as well as heavy professional work and duties, without *any secretary!*

Commenting on the reception of his book he remarks that it has received little attention from the Catholic Church in England. "Apart from a notice in the *Tablet*, not very good, I have been greeted with silence in this country. One of my most charming notices, however, was in the *Tablet* of New Zealand." And he was pleased with a review in a Catholic paper in America.

Later, in August, 1957, when it began to seem that he would never be able to make the trip to America, he wrote:

I will not bother you with a long wail, but June and July are usually crowded months academically, and I have been much harassed. Also, I have not been well recently, and arthritic trouble with the right hand has been a hindrance. Fortunately the hand does not object to tapping keys as much as to a pen; but I prefer a pen.

(Usually his letters, like his son's, are written in a fine hand.) The pen was waiting to be wielded every day.

Reading, writing and teaching, and academic affairs—and they can be the most deadly and corrosive of all the business of a don—consume time above all. Family and personal relationships involve an engagement that must be waged, won and lost each day, only to be neglected if life is no longer of consequence, the flag of surrender raised.

Inkling meetings were a release in the lives of all these men. The close society of Oxford permits the familiar association among similar souls, an essential anodyne to that alienation that is the besetting malaise of present days and to the frantic pace and bustle that has so little purpose yet is demanded by a sense of duty, fear and, perhaps above all, frustration. Yet these meetings shut the family out and have, in the long run, a debilitating effect.

Yet, on top, through and beyond all the dons' other concerns was their main and immediate reason for being, all else stemmed from it: they were teachers. The best descriptions of the teaching life, from both sides of the fire, come from John Lawlor and C.S. Lewis, whose letters, edited by his brother, form by far the best biography of their poor author. Lewis was in the first love affair; it was with dondom, with the Oxford where he had found his niche after long and difficult travail.

John Lawlor is a professor now, and his version of his first meeting with his tutor is good reporting. Lawlor met him first in 1936, when he came up to Oxford, where Lewis was at Magdalen. As usual, reading other accounts of coming up to Oxford—Emlyn Williams' *George* is among the best of them—Lawlor had a dream of the Sacred Town that jarred with the reality he encountered. He thought of dons lolling with pastel ties and sport jackets under the great chestnut tree of Balliol in apparent indolence, yet full of that effortless air of conscious superiority that Balliol tries too hard to inculcate. He tapped on the door of his tutor's rooms—Lewis' rooms. The sitting room looked out on Magdalen Grove, the other half of the suite commanded a view of the Cloister and, in the background, the incomparable Tower. The first tap on the door drew a bellowed "Come in," and there was his mentor for the next three years—red-faced, bald (the dark flop Coghill speaks of had gone), dressed in baggy jacket and trousers (no pastel tie!) and obviously in no mood to waste time, a permanent characteristic of Lewis. Opinions of Lewis from his students differ wildly. Christopher Tolkien praises him; others do not, found him touchy, offensive and cruel when they displeased him. He responded to, rather than evoked response from, many.

The tutorial ritual was invariable and very similar all over Oxford. The pupil, gowned, clutching his essay—once a week an essay of about three thousand words or more—sat on the edge of a chair or shapeless couch that seemed to have come with the building, long ago. After the reading, the tutor would begin. Ronald Knox remarked: "The prevailing attitude . . . was one of heavy disagreement with a number of things which the reader had not said."

Then the pupil, trying to defend his essay, would please or exasperate, annoy or bore the tutor. It was altogether a very demanding experience that Tolkien and his like followed nearly every day, besides being involved with themselves, their own writing and research—all basic food for the continuation of their teaching—and the drain upon them that the minds of the men they were educatng demanded. So their get-togethers were by way of release, and a necessary one.

A don has left a vivid impression of his daily round: awaking at seven-fifteen, rousing over a cup of tea, taking a brief walk to attend College chapel, breakfasting in company with others who had been at chapel with him, then a time answering notes and letters in his rooms until at nine he took up his pen and wrote resolutely for an hour. They were nearly all long hand writers, and it was amazing, as Owen Barfield has noted, that one draft, with revision, was generally enough to set their words for the printer.

At ten came the knock of the first student calling on his tutor, and the hungry generations began to tread him and his kind down. One of the most exhausting of all mental exercises lies in human encounter, even of a casual and general kind, when mind, eye and memory grope and search to make some sort of communion with another. This is far more so in the tutor-student relationship, where Encounter, Challenge and Response are the whole of the purpose.

There are generally four steady hours of tutorials before

lunch, after which the afternoon is spent in recreation and reflection. Around five two hours of tutorials may well begin again, and after dinner sometimes students come again for another three hours. "When they have gone and when I have glanced around the empty glasses and coffee cups and the chairs in the wrong places, I am glad enough to crawl into bed."

It was within the round of this kind of life that Tolkien lived. A poor man, living on his teaching and learning, he frequently examined and read papers as an external examiner for other universities. There was his family to raise, to send to private and expensive schools. Tolkien had little time to spare. The only exception to this program was one day a week when there were no students at all.

It has become a regular custom that Tolkien should drop in on me of a Monday morning and drink a glass. This is one of the pleasantest spots in the week. Sometimes we talk English School politics; sometimes criticize one another's poems; other days we drift into theology or "the state of the nation"; rarely we fly no higher than bawdy or puns. . . .*

Ten years later this same sort of meeting was going on, although the Inklings had begun to meet regularly long before this. They would meet generally fairly regularly but always casually. "The usual Thursday party did not meet . . . so I went up to Tolkien's. We had a very pleasant evening drinking gin and lime-juice and reading our recent chapters to each other—his from the new Hobbit and mine from *The Problem of Pain.*"**

Tolkien's path, and he was a regular don before he had got far into *The Lord of the Rings*, had been both set and beset. There was Saxony in the dim far background of his family past, his mother's ministry among the women of the Sultan of Zanzibar, his own roots in the soul of that most inland of English shires, Warwick, his birth on the high veld near Bloemfontein, his snatching by black Isaac, his running away from the snake through the tall dry

* W.H. Lewis, ed., *Letters of C.S. Lewis* (New York: Harcourt, Brace and World, 1966), p. 145.
** *Ibid.*, p. 172.

grass, the blaze and the sun of Africa, where events were moving toward the Dark Days to come, and his return home to Sarehole. There was his father's death and the solitary nature of his growing up, from sickly childhood into robust youth. The stories and the memories of his mother drew him toward tales and Faraway. The guardianship of the half-Spanish priest, Morgan, the conversion before he attended the Reformation establishment of King Edward's School, his mother's death and his years at Exeter College in Oxford, all drew him inexorably toward his rendezvous with Death, armed and yet open for what was to befall. The rearing and life of J.R.R. Tolkien, his infantry service and the war's end were all of one force that unified him within himself and were to lead him to the fate that he welcomed and the fame that surprised him in the years that came after. His popular fame began slowly with the publication of *The Hobbit;* his past is the invisible preface.

It was work, work, work for Tolkien during his Oxford years before World War II. He must have taken it amiss, although he would never admit it, that his life was far harder and more demanding than that of the other Inklings, save the physician Havard's perhaps.

One night in Cardiff—Tolkien was down there examining, as was his wont—he and Llewellyn, the Anglo-Saxon man there, talked and talked over pint after pint of beer as train after train, getting ever fewer as the night advanced, pulled out of Cardiff General for points east, including Oxford. "Llewellyn had quick darting eyes; did you ever notice that? He was a boxer, you know, used to fight for £5 in the Ring to get through College. . . ." Tolkien loves a yarn, a catch of a song; good company is welcome, any time that he is able to enjoy it.

He always watches the eyes. Roy Campbell's eyes attracted him. They were small and bright blue, Norse eyes, and he thought of Campbell as a Norseman, as he was in habit, persuasion and bellicosity. Tolkien loved all that. He and Lewis were in "The Burning Babe," one of their pubs, when Campbell came over, shabby, tousled, free as ever, and introduced himself. His heat and genius were a little too much for Lewis, but Tolkien loved him all the way, even for the violence that Campbell showed,

41

which was as much a part of him as his writing. It was like calling to like, Tolkien and Campbell. The welcome, the willingness to meet danger, even to court it, that were in Campbell, as much a part of him as his poetry and children's lore, were meat and drink to Tolkien, and in his reminiscences of the poet it is as if the don is going to a well where he would have liked to have drunk with Roy, although it could not be.

CHAPTER IV

THE HOBBITS OF TOLKIEN

Tolkien came to his fame by word of mouth. This is the ancient way of coming to it, by the telling of tales, and it still prevails in most of the world that still lies beyond the understanding of letters, let alone of print. Tolkien's fame by word of mouth long predates his telling of tales, however. It was by his lectures in class and his addresses before learned societies that his renown spanned the entire world of learning. Anglo-Saxon and the early Norse poetry have a strong beat and meter to them; all poetry and stories to be read aloud and remembered must possess these. And it was his readings before his classes in a language that they sensed but could not understand that him first remarkable. In his Gollancz Memorial lecture *"Beowulf:* The Monster and the Critics," which he delivered before the British Association in 1936, Tolkien clearly emerges at his scholarly and academic best, not only because of the substance of the lecture, but also because of the way that substance was delivered, so that people would listen. He begins with a "once upon a time" call to his hearers, trying to set them at their ease, professors and scholars all, by a gentle jibe at one of his predecessors in the Rawlinson Chair of Anglo-Saxon, which he occupied in 1936:

In 1864 the Reverend Oswald Cockayne wrote of

the Reverend Doctor John Bosworth, Rawlinsonian Professor of Anglo-Saxon: "I have tried to lend to others the conviction that I have long entertained that Dr. Bosworth is not a man so diligent in his special work as duly to read the books . . . which have been printed in our old English, or so-called Anglo-Saxon tongue. He may do very well for a professor."

From the gentle humor of this beginning, almost in the same breath, and this is a grand way to rivet the attention of an audience—and Tolkien always had an audience in mind—he moved into an attack, threw down the gauntlet, shouted his brag. If there were a modern Cockayne, he said, he would similarly accuse another Bosworth of not reading the books about the books that were written in the Anglo-Saxon tongue. Small wonder it would be if this were so, for the critics and the scholars have been caught up in the web of their own obfuscation so that they have forgotten what all their scholarship was about in the first place. As a result, "The books are nearly buried."

Some of the critics had not even read the *Beowulf* about which they spent all their time writing footnotes and engaging in controversy. While Tolkien confesses with ironic humility that he has not read all the critical work they have produced, he has read enough to realize that while Beowulfiana is rich in several departments, it is woefully and specially poor in criticism.

This was the rousing beginning of a lecture that has become famous, that has been issued in paperback along with his later Andrew Lang lecture and a story, *Leaf by Niggle*, which he wrote long before it was published in an obscure, scholarly Catholic journal, *The Dublin Review*. It appeared in 1947 and should have remained there.

The more Tolkien is read in relation to his place and time and background, the more clear it becomes that he wrote for the word to be heard. He read aloud, as we know now from the Inklings, both *The Hobbit* and *The Lord of the Rings*. It was the word that got around, first around a fire in an Oxford College or pub, that brought the stories together, that even explains much of their form, for his readers were members mostly of the English School of Oxford, or related to it, so there was challenge and response to all he said. Challenge is best met head on, and the cordial or begrudging, even bored sometimes, response having been sought and obtained encouraged him to pursue his enormous and most erudite task of subcreation. Moreover, since these men came together first of all in friendship because of their likenesses, the great feature of Tolkien's work and thought were given full rein.

He had someone in mind when he attempted his relation, someone specific, even if someone composite. Every storyteller fixes his eye on an audience and keeps his eye on it, otherwise the tale wavers, does not relate to his task, which is to share an experience, a philosophy even, through his tale. His purpose is frustrated unless the tale holds, is accepted as a story first of all. Every story must start off as an "in" story, and from Coleridge's Ancient Mariner's yarn of the Albatross to Hemingway's "Fifty Grand" they are.

Tolkien never had to fear that hostile criticism based on willful ignorance or rejection that might have discouraged him in other learned company. Rather, he was excited by this constant encounter to spread the Word among them, too much for some of them though it might be. Every writer is by nature objective and lonely; the greater the writer, the more he is removed. This alienation is a part of the price of Art, and the greatest danger that can come to any writer is to hear the siren and seductive invitation to join the gang, to become involved in the game. It needs a great belief in the value of one's art to reject the bid. Many do not have it and are to that degree diminished. It is hard to think that this seduction ever visited Tolkien; he has always been his own man and has suffered for it, but that is the way it goes. He has used his learning and his creativity to the full and pays for it, for all his jolly bonhomie.

It is with a sense of unbelief that the young and unsure realize that among the scholars and the men whom they most admire there is a sense of commitment, to some sort of religion, to some belief that governs their action. Many a one of them, in this day and age, is "a thorough-going super-naturalist." Owen Barfield, around Tolkien, was profoundly religious, and so were Hugo Dyson, C.S. Lewis, Charles Williams, Gervase Mathew, his doctor,

Havard. These were prime among the Inklings, so Tolkien was free to develop his theme among them in an understanding air.

Religion is the basis of good fairy stories: this is so in *The Hobbit*. The fairy story is a recovery of what we have lost, or dreamed of as having lost, in the past. So we press onward and deeper down to seek the quiet kindness that lay about us in our infancy, to have around again that love of yore. Children cherish this above all. Whoever denies it to them is damned; he has sinned against his nature, denied and broken a universal law. A love free of passions, a family love, this children require, a love that belongs because we are part of it, sharing in what we all were once and can be once again for always. This grasp of heaven almost daily slackens with growing up, is forgotten and denied in our pride, youth, passion, sensual perception and strength, passes out of our grip, yet peers out of the windows of the eyes of all, the more out of those who are sick, old and forsaken. It is when that need is quite dead that men are mad; madness above all is alienation, a descent into Hell, the only Hell. Tolkien is leery of passion, as well he might be, as well might all.

Yet men cannot see themselves in the heroic situations that are the stuff of Fantasy—on a white horse charging a castle full of villainy, as the fearless agent of a country's stratagem in a time of nuclear crisis—unless there is a climate for such telling such as Tolkien enjoyed and such as the present age affords for moral tales bedizened with bawdy and the kitchen sink, the bathroom and the bed. Tales need a time and place to grow in the attention of an audience, and Tolkien had this ready-made, alert and about him. There can be no chasm between the marvels and the reader; here Tolkien succeeds. His Hobbit is both a bridge and a being more like Man than are the heroic, familiar and mock-human counterparts that appear in adventure stories. Moreover, the Hobbit is more English than a Cockney, more of a tyke than a Yorkshireman, as chaw-bacon as a Dorset, as indolent as any rustic would like to be, more of a human than if he were one, as *petit-bourgeois* as if he caught the 8:15 commuter train and the wife prided herself on her peanut fudge and casseroles. There are Hobbit recipes now; soon there will be a Gandalf doll, jolly Hobbit songs—and Tolkien relishes the lot.

They are very like us, the creatures, the Hobbits: relations. There is nothing cute or minuscule, gossamer or twinkletoe about their looks. Tolkien has them about three feet tall, give or take an inch, and they are very dull. Outsiders, humans, refer to them as Halflings, as Australians call Britishers Pommies and the rest of the British call the Welshmen Taffs. They steer from the trouble of Man, tend their own garden. And they are good at it, especially at growing good things to eat. Tolkien never condescends to them: he likes them, more is the pity some critics think, but he would not be Tolkien otherwise. His affection for the Hobbit sprang naturally from the well of the nature of this complicated man. He turns to them with a chortling relief that can be jarring.

Hobbit habitations used to be in burrows underground, and Tolkien suggests that their name might stem from this, from what might have been the Anglo-Saxon word for a holebuilder, *holbytla*. Edmund Wilson in his derisory, spluttering, yet somehow welcome and refreshing review of Tolkien's subcreation, "Oo, Those Awful Orcs," remarks that the word "hobbit," with its rural connotations, might well be an amalgam of hob (=companion of) and rabbits, because of the burrowing and their proclivity for nibbling.

Wilson's blast at Tolkien needs to be read, for it blows away a lot of the nonsense, the fatuous and fulsome adulation that has so befouled the spare, taut, iron tale of *The Lord of the Rings* and *The Hobbit*. The latter, the first and recommended introduction to the greater Trilogy, the primer to *The Lord of the Rings*, is responsible for his swipe. Really, *The Hobbit* can be the worst introduction to *The Lord of the Rings;* it can put people off, has done so to many. It is an important part of the Tolkien canon, yet it remains a children's book. The horns of Elfland are only faintly sounding; children can romp through it, and so can many grown-ups, but, for most, they can do it more easily after they have read Tolkien's master work: the Trilogy.

The Hobbit lends itself to folly, to misinterpretation, because Tolkien here, in his first essay, did not write up to his might; he even wrote down for children, a mistake that he admits, even if he also denies it. There is a too-jolly air about it, the thought is spared as if children were in mind,

46

the jocularity against which all such Englishmen as he must beware is all too evident. Tolkien prattles, even if children were the audience he had in mind, and the book suffers: prattle is always wrong. Tolkien realized this: "All children's books are on a strict judgment poor books. Books written entirely for children are poor even as children's books."

Many find Tolkien barred to them because *The Hobbit* has repelled them. The beginning of *The Lord of the Rings* is too full of hobbitry for many. If the tale started at the beginning of the Quest and the preface and footnotes, appendixes and most of the verse were cut out, the book would win truer friends, get better acceptance, but then the whole of Tolkien would be diminished: it is better to take it as he wishes.

The Hobbit, even when read to children, has adults in mind. And even if there's too much of the schoolboy chortle in it, the book maintains the formal and necessary structure that Tolkien has laid down for the fairy story, be it great or small, for there is Fantasy in it, which is the purest of the art forms, the hardest to realize, the most free and wide-swinging to use once it is mastered, and that's very rarely—by Lewis Carroll maybe and by some of the gospel-makers. Escape from oppressive and meaningless detail follows as a bonus from the mastery of Fantasy, and the recovery of the true perspective comes too, allowing the vision to emerge rightly, not from an angle, as from this bent world. Above all, and finally, comes Consolation, the joy of a happy ending that goes on forever, long beyond the end of the story. Implicit in Fantasy is the promise of the consolation of a happy death, of Union with all that is good, until the end of time.

There is nothing fancy about the Hobbits, on the contrary. Would that there were. Their realism is that of the man around the corner who sings on Sunday morning as he polishes his car. They watch the antics of humans when at their heroics with something of comic resignation. They are involved in these carryings-on, as clerks and fraternity men are caught up in causes. Tolkien, almost despite himself, shows his almost dazed affection for them by giving them an Englishry wherein he and his Oxford company share. To award Englishry is the greatest compliment that

Tolkien could afford a creature. The English are the most arrogant of people, but, pitched to their low key and civilized, their arrogance is their most exasperating and delightful trait.

The Shire of the Hobbits is no Never-Never Land, no Big Rock Candy Mountain; it is better than that, to Tolkien, to his Hobbits. It is a bit of England he has willed them, and that is something he would not find in his nature to do to anybody who was not born within it. He is a most intolerant and conservative man, as the English are, in the end. The Hobbits are all sorts and degrees, rich and poor, upper, middle and lower classes, but Hobbit lower classes are forelock-tugging yokels as divorced from their own dreams and agony as the Irish creatures of Somerville and Ross, the grinning, bowing, house servant-slaves of the old South, the quaint little 'tween-maids of the Victorian ménage, the cottagers who hedged and thatched and plowed for the gentry while their children went into domestic service in the Big House—all, all are in a Hell that their masters designed for them, and yet most of them believe that that is good for them, or that that is all they are good for. Tolkien has no vision for the poor; few of his class did, and they became outsiders. The class structure is apparent all through Tolkien's description of Hobbit life. They are nonintellectual, as he is in this day and age. He shares a lot of their tastes, or he would if he could. There is no understanding or appreciation of new-fangled ways. They would no more give house room to an abstract painting than they would read a Westron text if they didn't have to. He places them, all his characters, in an archaic society where the song resounded:

God bless the Squire and his relations
And keep us all in our proper stations.

There are never any women in Tolkien's story, any more than there are poor. They are of no concern to him in his relation, and it is just as well; for if there were, there would be no end of his kingdom of the mind. He did enough, more than any other man in his chosen theme, and what lies beyond was beyond him. Tolkien needs to be read for what he offers and must not be judged for failing to deliver what he could not give, any more than

Spenser, or Powell, or Albee.

The Hobbit was subcreated during the thirties from what Tolkien calls the Red Book of Westmarch, the Hobbit book of record. He is infuriating in his meticulous matching up of the time of his creation with the real time of history. It bewilders. He is serious about it. No wonder heads reel, eyes ache, minds falter through his genealogical and historical convolutions; none of them has any real bearing on the tale. And *The Hobbit* sounds the first note, quaveringly, charmingly, too cutely as Tolkien admits, of the great theme of the Trilogy. *The Lord of the Rings.* There is no better literary, critical or historical introduction to Tolkien's major work than this slight volume, but that does not mean it is the key for the general reader: not at all. Like the appendices and prefaces that Tolkien has provided for his major work, it can both bewilder and repel. He has encircled his whole subcreation with learning of a kind that presupposes all too much background in a general reader. *The Hobbit* is simple, all too simple to lead to *The Lord of the Rings.* It is a book that stands alone, *sui generis,* but it is more important and gives far more value when it is considered as the genesis, the seminal relation of the Trilogy. But the wriggle of the fetus does not necessarily have to be observed in order to understand the action of a Man. The contrary is generally the case, save for specialists. So it is with *The Hobbit.*

There and Back Again is the sub-title of *The Hobbit,* and it is the tale of a Quest. Bilbo Baggins, a country squire of a Hobbit, is snug and content in his handsome well-furnished burrow, surrounded by his creature comforts. A bachelor, he esteems his comforts even more than most of his comfort-loving kin. The wizard Gandalf, at this stage of the subcreation almost a comic scarecrow, comes to his door one day, followed by thirteen dwarves of whom he is the finger man, and inveigles Bilbo into leaving his gentleman Hobbit's residence at Bag End and going along with them to seek and recover the dwarf treasure lifted from them in the past by an evil dragon. Thorin Oakenshield is the dwarf leader, descendant of dwarf kings.

Bilbo, for some reason he never understood, agrees to join them—after they have accepted more than heartily his hospitality, eaten him out of all his ample provender, slept all over his rooms and shown a certain disdain for Hobbits generally—when it comes to action. There is action all right, following Bilbo's joining the Quest. Trolls capture them and burn them, almost; goblins chase them; giant spiders enmesh them in their saliva; a king of elves incarcerates them. But they get to the dragon's den and lift the treasure. There follows the Battle of the Five Armies wherein Thorin Oakenshield of the dwarf kingly blood is killed, although victory is won. Bilbo, honored among dwarves for his valiance and comfort, returns to Bag End, loaded with the treasure the dwarves pile upon him from their recaptured hoard, just in time to save his household belongings from being auctioned off, for he is presumed to be dead, having been away so long and so mysteriously. Any Hobbit who leaves the Shire is regarded as odd to begin with; they are regular homebodies, the Hobbits, and it is with a sigh of something less than joy that they accept Bilbo back among them, far wealthier than ever, and return to him his belongings—some, such as his set of silver spoons, never get back to him. So all is well again for Bilbo. He should live happily on to his end, and Hobbits live a long time, about twice as long as men.

But there is some unfinished business, and this is the nub of it, the lead that has brought Tolkien to the great work of the Trilogy. During the Quest Bilbo has a most unpleasant encounter with Gollum, a creature who cannot bear the light. Gollum nearly kills Bilbo, who is saved alive by the ancient device of the Riddle Game. During the danger of Gollum, crawling through the dark of goblin mines, Bilbo accidently finds a gold ring, which he pockets, but it is the Ring, it turns out, around which Gollum's degradation and life revolve. Bilbo tries on the Ring for size and finds it gives him the power to become unseen, to be able to hide from his enemies. Among the dwarves, intent on the recovery of their treasure, this Ring seems of little consequence, but it turns out that the fate of the world hangs from it. Gandalf knows Bilbo has a ring; that is all that it is to Bilbo, a very queer sort of ring, but a ring. Frodo, Bilbo's nephew and heir, hero-to-be, knows about it too; Bilbo tells him, but that is all. The significance of the Ring lies beyond the understanding of all during *The Hobbit.* It works on the mind, including the mind of Tolkien, who only gradually realizes its significance. The power of the Ring is evil; it bestows the corruption of absolute power on the wearer and gradually the wearer will want that. Absolute power can be used to prevent wrong, but what power can control the power of the Ring that is stronger than its wearer? Only a perfect being can wear the ring, but such a being would not need it, and were Middle-earth, the place of Tolkien's story, people with perfect beings it would be Never-Never Land, not earth, nor would the rulers of that place be men.

Gradually, in working out this theme, with pleasure and thought and deep satisfaction, through fourteen years that encompassed World War II, his passing from the prime of his life, the growing up of his family, the dying of some of his friends, the increasing responsibilities of his academic office, Tolkien worked on this great universal theme and out of it came *The Lord of the Rings.* The common elements of both the Trilogy and *The Hobbit* have suggested to some that *The Hobbit* is but an offshoot of or a preliminary diversion to *The Lord of the Rings*, and there is some merit in this reflection; for while there is no suggestion in *The Hobbit* of man's unique possession, the free will that contains both his doom and salvation, as he chooses, there is the beginning of a suggestion of the significance and order of the Cosmos when Gandalf gently reproaches Bilbo when the Quest is over:

> You don't really think, do you, that all your adventures and escapes were managed by mere luck, just for your sole benefit? You are a very fine person, Mr. Baggins, and I am very fond of you; but you are only quite a little fellow in a wide world after all!

Moreover the "naked will and courage" that both Bilbo and his development in his nephew, Frodo, possess are those Norse attributes that Tolkien refers to earlier as being altogether admirable, in that very phrase, in his 1936 British Academy Lecture.

The rather jolly virtues of the Hobbits, couched often in the language of *Chums, The Boy's Own Paper* or even *The Magnet*, the schoolboy weeklies that were in their prime in Tolkien's youth, are raised to solemn magnificence when it is realized that these virtues endow their possessors with the power to face and subdue the terrible and soul-destroying opposition of the Evil that besets them. There is none of *The Boy's Own Paper* about Sauron, the Ringwraiths, Trolls, Orcs or Gollum. It is the choice to face or not to face Evil, it is the reluctant choice that raised Bilbo and more so his heir, Frodo, above even great Beowulf. This echoes memories of War, when unlettered, fornicating, foul-mouthed Tommies were heroes, pure and simple, on occasion. Even Evelyn Waugh, purged of his folly and giving up at last his vain courting to be accepted, comes to some of this wisdom in his last and best book, the trilogy of *The Sword of Honour*.

The very fact that Bilbo, when he had Gollum at his mercy in *The Hobbit* after he had won the Riddle Game and had come by the Ring, showed his mercy and spared the wretched creature was to turn to Bilbo's advantage and to glorious gain under Frodo. Their virtue spared Bilbo and later Frodo from the ultimate power of the Ring when they possessed it.

Most conversation and argument among the readers of *The Hobbit* and the Trilogy are centered upon irrelevancies. There is even some general impression among them that it is a philological fun game: to trace on the maps the Quests and wanderings, to identify the Bay of Belfalas with perhaps Colwyn Bay of the Present-earth, Eriador with the Ceredigion of Wales, the Misty Mountains with the Black Mountains of Brecon, Gondor with Morganwg, Rhudair with Radyr, Mirkwood with the Black Country, the Shire with the bosky parts of the County of Warwick. Many readers are relieved that there is nothing they can discover that is relevant to their condition in Tolkien's work: it is escape literature of a charming kind to them, as *Alice in Wonderland* was to generations before them until Jonathan Miller showed a reluctant audience of millions of television viewers otherwise. Miller exposed the terrors of the human mind that teem in Alice; Tolkien reveals the power and dignity that reside in Man, however hidden they may be, as they are, most of the time, and he does it through a little Hobbit, Frodo, who is Man in essence, more than man.

CHAPTER V

THE TALE OF THE RING

Certain simple facts emerge from the Hobbits at the time of the Ring that serve as a frame or as a background, saving the reader from the days or a lifetime of research mong the runes, looking for facts where they are not, where seeking only reveals ignorance and where each discovery of the reader's own opens up new vast darknesses. A stone is turned to discover its mineral significance in structure, never to start a wing.

The place of the great Hobbit action is Middle-earth, something like a Europe of these days. But instead of a channel between Britain and the rest of that Earth, there was the barrier of the Misty Mountains, and Britain is Wales, with the heart of England in the middle of the principality.

It was in the northwest of Tolkien land, on the wrong—east—side of the Mountains and in the upper vales of the river Anduin that the Hobbits used to dwell, the Red Book of Westmarch recounts. There had been Dark Ages, then, before those that were to come. The Tale of Years, as Tolkien tells it, had seen the gradual overwhelming of the forces of Good by the hordes of Evil, as if an Eden had become rank and jungled. The race of gentle bettermen, the men of Numenor, had declined and passed away, too good for the dirty world that followed and folded them. Sauron was the Lord of Evil, full of lore, Ring-corrupted, rotten. Saruman was the scholar-scientist gone wrong, beguiled into evil by his desire to control Man; first it was to be for Man's own good, then as creatures of his will, for he knew better than they: that is the final state of blasphemy.

Sauron is a most relevant character, and revealing, too. He sought for his fell purpose the power of the Rings. These, which came originally from the depths of the earth, were greater than all the riches in the earth. Into the forging and tempering went all the sweating hopes of those who owned them, and even elves sweat, although it seems as if they only glow. There were four sorts of Power Rings, all wrought by the eleven smiths, save the one Great Lord of Rings, Sauron's own. Sauron got into his hands the nine Rings of Man and made the Ring bearers the Ringwraiths, his most dreadful arm, fallen men. Some of the seven that the dwarves possessed were consumed by fire-belching dragons, and the others were possessed by Sauron, taking away the dwarves' power and sorely diminishing yet bettering their state; dwarves, the cantankerous creatures, were better off without them. The three rings of the elven folk were beyond Sauron. They had remained with the best of men's kindred and gone with them beyond the White Towers and the Sea, out of his grasp, as the elves were ever. (The elves and men of Tolkien's relation are his poorest subcreation, save for his women. Man's Fate is more his concern than Man, and the elves betray his wistful thinking.) The one great Ring of Sauron, lost since Isildur the Elf has perished in the river, found and worshiped by fallen Gollum, unwittingly became Bilbo's power that would have sickened him to death but for the mercy he had shown, bound together the Company in their search for its destruction, for it was the Ring that gave Sauron his power, and it could only be destroyed by being cast into the Fire Mountain of Mordor.

Sauron, in his final preparation against the coming age when Man should rule the Middle-earth again unless he prevailed, was prepared to march but for the Ring. He needed that above all.

Appalled when he realizes the awful significance of the Ring that Bilbo has bequeathed him, the young Hobbit, Frodo, turns to Gandalf for aid, tries to make the good wizard take the Ring. Gandalf, who has learned that possession of that Ring leads to worse than even Good can overcome, to veritable transubstantiation into Devil, refuses, for all the ringing temptation; Galdalf has a pity that borders on the divine, "the desire of strength to do good."

Frodo flees with the Ring to save the Shire from Sauron's devastation, for now Sauron knows who has the Ring. Gandalf goes his own way to summon aid for

Frodo, now on his way. Frodo sets out from the Shire with his servant, Sam. Sam, Frodo, Merry and Pippin, companions of his youth—they would all have gone to a minor English Public School in Tolkien's day—begin their Quest to destroy the Ring that only Frodo knows, though Sam senses something of it. To Merry and Pippin it all seems rather like a lark.

Dangers beset them almost as soon as they leave home. Frodo makes mistakes and is wounded, but at every danger he chooses to go on.

With every choice, venturing further and further into paths unknown, into danger ever increasing, into times more ominous, the counter against Evil, and against the Ring, becomes more and more strong, makes Sauron, and Saruman the fallen wizard who has entered the lists against the Good of Frodo, more and more violent.

Tribulations beset the Hobbits, dangers and doubts besides. But they reach Rivendell, the Bastion of the West, the last Home east of the Sea, with man Strider, their guide and guard; now Man's own kind enters the theme of the story, becomes the warp and the woof of it. Elrond Halfelven calls the Council that decides upon the destruction of the Lord of the Rings, Sauron himself.

This means that the fellowship of the Free People must venture into the very depth of Evil's land, and this Company of the Ring, Hobbits three, men two, elf, dwarf and Gandalf, set out on a hunter's moon. Strider becomes known as Aragorn, King of the West, and Boromir, the other man, kingly also, heir to Denethor, Lord of the Tower of Guard. The Ring possessed him for a while, and in his sin he succumbed to the power of it. Frodo faced the Orcs before Aragorn arrived to aid, finding only Boromir dying, rueing his fall.

Frodo alone, save for faithful Sam, struggles on and spares the life of Gollum, remembering Gandalf before he became executioner:

Deserves death! . . . Many that live deserve death. And some die that deserve life. Can you give them to them? Then be not too eager to deal out Justice.

Frodo falls; Sam, common, comical, loving Sam, as common as a Tommy, carries on alone into the pit of Hell on earth, Mordor. There, while the Company of the Ring wages a battle with all its might against Sauron as a diversion, Frodo Redivivus proceeds with Sam to the fiery pinnacle to cast in the Ring. At that point Frodo falters at the temptation of the Ring and might have fallen save for Gollum, whom he had spared. Gollum, alive because of Frodo's clemency, snatches the Ring from Frodo's reluctant hand and dies with it in the earth-deep crevasse of the mountain, slipping to perdition just when the Ring was in his grasp.

Then Aragorn shows he is made to be King, for he redeems his Company from death with his gift of Healing, the mark of a King.

All seems well, but Frodo has lost his living for his kin. While Sam, Pippin and Merry gleefully contemplate their return to the Shire, where Sam is to flourish and weather for years as the Mayor, Frodo is no more for this world; he has transcended hobbitry. His wounds will not altogether mend again in this life, and he bids farewell to Sam, wishing he were returning with him:

> But I have been too deeply hurt, Sam. I tried to save the Shire, and it has been saved, but not for me. It must be often so Sam when things are in danger: someone has to give them up, to lose them that others may keep them.

He sails away with Bilbo to the Haven of the West, their Avalon.

There, in the Trilogy, is the struggle of this earth and beyond. The most heart-rending of the enemies of Man are those that have fallen away from Man's estate, the Ringwraiths. Some men will always fall away, for this dismaying flaw is as indissoluble from virtue as the brine is from the sea, and when the brine is extracted, something vital has gone out.

Yet Man has the power to love, to give and to fight for it, which is possessed by no other creature. The near-sanctity of the elves, the benevolence of the Hobbits, who possess all the great virtues of courage, steadfastness, loyalty and choice, the dour, truculent fidelity of the dwarves are pale beside, if more palatable and easier to understand than, the infinite and various qualities of Man.

Therefore Gandalf demands Man's aid in his crusade for restoration of his Man, Aragorn, who is infused with some of the goodness of the elves though within his genes lies the destructive potential that has crashed Gandalf's hopes for Man before. Only under Man does Middle-earth make sense; it was all intended for him and will continue to be so until the world's end, when he shall encompass his own destruction—as he has so nearly done in the past, though never more than now—or reach the end of the world and stride into what lies beyond.

Man's fate is so vast in its complication, promise and past, and so difficult to comprehend since we are part of it, that its contemplation has fallen into exegesis, and only now and then, as in the sayings of Christ, has its full nature been envisaged. It contains the root and the sum of all creation's drive, and this it is that makes it so entrancing, exhilarating and perilous. And such is Man: he would rather balance on the tightrope of his own creation, razor-thin and sagging in the middle, over the abysmal valley of his own folly, than walk in safety starting meadowlarks. It is in danger and in the times that most try his soul that he flourishes. He is born to trouble as sparks fly upward. When his situation is most impossible, when he has lost all control, save perhaps over an individual being here and there, then he triumphs most, just as in the three centuries of turmoil that came with the Breaking of the Faith in Italy his spirit has soared into high work of creation. It is to danger and turmoil, when Man realizes that the Good is threatened, that he responds; the challenge is the spur. Moreover, and this is Tolkien's great contribtion to the canon of supernatural literature, no more need there be even hope of a happy ending. The decision to struggle on when defeat seems inevitable is the true glory of Man that Tolkien has brought forward again from the great Norse ideal.

For weal or woe Gandalf was committed to Man because his sense and wisdom unerringly led him to the conclusion that Man was the heart of the matter and needed all the help he could get.

Aragorn, who is Strider, the Valiant of the tale, is almost too good to be human, he has some of the qualities of a noble horse. Man needs more than a dash of pity to be his exciting self; a sharp taste for sin must be in him too, if he is to be wholly vital.

Yet, above all, Gandalf has a love for Man that only saints—good servants are saints—can acquire. The apostle Paul had it for the Galatians, Patrick, maybe, for the Irish, Gandhi for the people of India. And somehow the soul of Man responds to that love more fully and more beautifully than to any other.

The flower will open its petals to the sun, a stone will show its many-faceted beauty in the turn of the weather, the sea will bare its bosom to the moon, and all nature can rise in a carillon on occasion, but Man's love does more than stretch itself under caress, more than show the brilliance of his many-sided mind, more than sing loud the hallelujahs. He can freely give himself, often to death and worse, for others and for justice's sake, and all for love and nothing for reward. Man's response to love can shame the giver of it, so that the wise offer it charily. And since Gandalf knew all this, he was hooked on the Quest more surely than the whale.

CHAPTER VI

CRAFT AND ART

The whole core of Tolkien's work is man-centered, and spiritual thereby, free of the apologetics that are scarcely concealed in the works of such writers—to whom he is wrongly linked—as C.S. Lewis and Charles Williams. Tolkien's work is the very nub, the heart of spiritual fantasy; the others are but fatty tissue compared to his.

Tolkien makes his subcreation so down-to-earth, in Man's world, that it is tedious for some who are bored, for example, by his maps and diagrams of Middle-earth, the trails of the Hobbits and the journey of the Quest. Middle-earth is where the action is, and there is plenty of that, and suspense too as the Fellowship of the Ring advances into the territory of the Enemy. Sometimes Tolkien contrives moments of real terror, as when Pippin drops a stone, sending it rattling away to break the ominous stillness of patrol, or when the Ringwraiths look down like basilisks upon the struggle of the little band. There is something of the elemental earth when Treebeard, older than Forests, comes to succor the band, and Tolkien's eye for the lay of the land is revealed in his writing to be better than that in any book of strategy or exploration. There is so much action piled on action, so intricate is the pattern of the narrative, yet somehow the woods remain clear in spite of the trees, which is as the author intended for all his preoccupation with the thousands of details that make up the tale.

Art of any kind must bear relation, must be a hand put forth, be a flag raised, a signal of distress. Frodo, the hero Hobbit, is Tolkien's relation, one that can be taken as far as the reader is able to take it. Tolkien cavalierly dismisses requests to elucidate the implications of his theme: that is asking too much. He turns away from it and busies himself with elvish lore and the like with obvious relief. He is like Dante of a dream who, having borne the dreamer to the very brink of Inferno, shown him the hell of it, when asked what the dreamer should do about it, shrugs his shoulders and does not answer. After all, it is the dreamer's dream, to do with what he can or will.

Whatever the reader makes of it, the simplest joy that comes out of Tolkien is from the first reading. It is with the question that this reading raises, with the commentaries, reviews, articles and footnotes, that the niggle starts, only to begin to itch furiously when engaged in Tolkien dialogue with others who have read his work. By this time a lesson is suspected, so many will back away: a lesson is the last thing they were looking for. Escape was in their minds, escape among the elves and in the trees. Truth is the last thing the readers seek, let alone to practice, save for practical purposes, where it serves well. Man dislikes the Truth; he never has believed in it enough to espouse it, nor will he ever.

Tolkien urges that his work is meant to be read for enjoyment. He urges this and protests it all too much. He should not be asked these questions about the meaning of his work; they are questions that should not be put to any artist, for artists give no answers. They should follow the practice of another writer, an artist in other ways: "Never apologize, never explain." By his very nature an artist is unable to explain his work, either to his own or to succeeding generations. His only explanation lies within his work and what the world makes of it; only his work can speak for him, and, in the end, it will prevail. Popularity of good art in the right season, when the author is still alive to respond to it, is always for the wrong reason, as it is in Tolkien's case, save perhaps among the young, and that is because they are not old enough: their Mordor is still over the hill; their morning is at seven, all can be right with the world.

The greatest virtue of Tolkien's art, which he shares with all gifted like him, in all the arts, is that appreciation of his work deepens in relation to the need or desire of the reader. "The Night Watch" of Rembrandt is a pleasure to see, even for a few moments as one passes through the gallery in the Low Country. But the more one realizes what Rembrandt was faced with in those times, the more the painting extends and welcomes, so that even the figures change and become Knights and Shriners.

Tolkien always aimed to give pleasure to his readers. Otherwise the Inklings would not have endured his reading over the years. He aimed to catch the reader's imagination, eye and mind, for otherwise he is talking to himself or to others like him, blaming the world, taking in the washing of another who tubs his.

Man's life depends upon a series of choices that he must make himself. In the same way he must make what he can or wishes of Tolkien. It is upon his acceptance or rejection of choices that his future depends, and it is upon the embrace of the wrong ones that prosperity generally lies on this earth.

Tolkien has sometimes a naughty, donnish, Socratic habit of responding to one question with another, especially to a question from those who would have him find an answer for them, something that they must find alone. Because of the cults that have begun to spring up around his name—the Tolkien craze—and because of the pontificatory and exegetical pronouncements of critics such as Wilson, there are many who are repelled or otherwise turn away from him. And among these are the very best, ones who would read him most.

Tolkien has been pricked by the uncouth and stupid, to answer them in terms of their own coin, further bewildering some who would find an answer in him. The chief matter of Tolkien is often neglected and rejected when the grand simplicity of the whole is torn up by malevolent or committed scholars and gaping admirers. For years now Oxford has been rife with jibes about his work, and among his disciples there are some of the dreariest critics, gowned Boy Scouts and halflings with stings on their tongues when they have no tails. It is the allegory of the man and his tower that Tolkien propounded in his address on *Beowulf* to the British Academy all over again. This time, alas, it is his own grand structure that is under the fragmentation process, not only in the day-to-day comment, but in exegetical essays and dissertations too.

The most popular theme in the literature of the West is Sacrifice. Man is drawn to it, cherishes it, passes it by. In the American Western, on film and in stories such as *Shane*, the hero is the cowpoke Christ who rides into town, lonely and obscure, and by his sole example delivers the people for a while from the Power of the Dog, the Bankers or the Bandits—as in *The Magnificent Seven*. The Japanese genesis of that film, stretching back to the Samurai tradition, extends the relevance. The same theme, Sacrifice, runs through that most popular form of literature, the detective story, where Harper or Sam Spade, remote, obscure, rejected, brings justice and mercy into a shabby or fancy world in the teeth of organized society. Sherlock Holmes remained the most recognized character in all of English fiction for half a century.

Yet to match the Hegelian theme to *Shane*, as has been done, to talk about the *leit-motif* in Sam Spade, to become a Baker Street Irregular and find in the library of Sherlock Holmes a philosophic reason for his *Sign of Four* denotes an esoteric interest that delights the few but bewilders the many who feel uneasy and embarrassed because they read Chandler, MacDonald or Doyle for fun. So it is with Tolkien at first and at a later superficial reading. And yet Tolkien himself is so full of lore, and of mischief of a kind, that it spills over in his appendices, notes and

61

references. Moreover as a teacher, and he was a born and a great one, he must respond to the questions his works raise among those who learn from him. But his answers pose further questions, which he answers exhaustively with references, so that the eager student's mind stretches. The common reader, who is of all the one that matters, finds himself poring over the maps of Mordor, tracing the arrows toward Haradwaith and seeking for the pass over the Misty Mountains through which the Hobbits made it to their Shire. Then the general joy may turn to particular pleasure, for the few *aficionados* who trace the routes and seek the roots of words. The maps that are appended to *The Lord of the Rings* were made by hand; the detail is so tiny that a magnifying glass, enlarging the details, fails to give a bird's eye view, and that is what the common reader must obtain if he is to go further than the rivers, roads, fords and forests of Middle-earth. He needs only a general idea of them, and of the tongue and the time that ran in Tolkien's mind when he created them, and should seek for no more.

Tolkien can no more be simple about this than be untrue to his vocation and the years that went into the forming of it. Yet through knowledge only can the Truth come, and love with it, and Tolkien ennobles Man, honors him, more than any other writer of creative spiritual fiction.

CHAPTER VII

MAN FOR TOLKIEN

Man is hard to handle. A free agent, often he rejects what he thinks of us as the Good, let alone good wizards like Gandalf—good men. For as long as Man lives Nature and all beyond relate to him. But there is something in Man, divine and diabolic, that rejects this. When his malign desire embraces Nature, it is to subdue it and harness it to his will. When his good desire woos it, it is often to escape his manhood and be subject within it, to pull Nature over him like a blanket. The body's chemistry, land, sea, sun and sky are all related this way or that. What is eternal in Man's mind contains this record, but it overlords it with a vain and brave attempt, encompassing catastrophe, to break free of the tutelage that is built within, the Authority, to relate or not to relate as the will moves—not as his memory relates—not to share in love but to control or to cower. Man leaps from ice floe to ice floe, from hummock to tussock, to avoid facing the record and living by it. He rejects the surrender of his will, and his rejection is the cause of much of his woe, and the world's woe. Yet without this free will of his he would not be. This is what makes him a man: the dearest and the most dangerous of creatures. Tolkien knows it too well for comfort.

Man's ego requires that he bestride, control, realize the human condition, but that Man will not do, for long, anyway. If he does, the herd destroys him. Tolkien spells out this in his tale. There is the joy and thrill of it, the reason, whether they know it consciously or not, that the young of this generation embrace him. Never before has Man been so ashamed of his record; he cowers from it. And the young, seeking challenge, looking for the rock, probing their elders more and more to discover it, find only mush, are given pablum to grow fat and sassy on when they seek a stone to hold on to, to climb up from.

The dragons and these "Awful Orcs" that so offended Edmund Wilson in his derisory yet salutary review in *The Nation* seem but a bored don's blunder to many critics. But always in heroic legend the heroes have been dragon-slayers. Dragons are no idle fancy; they are a potent force that man's imagination has created out of his past. Man's image of himself changes with each generation. Tolkien makes the symbol of the dragon stand for Evil, for Evil does not change with the style; it always retains cognizance, even becomes horribly real, as, for example, when fire-belching tanks lurch over the dirty ground of battle amid flashes, screams and howls overhead toward the resolute few glum heroes of the Infantry, men with weapons in their hands and nothing else, save within, to stop the squealing, treading, clanking, baleful progress of the armor.

Tolkien relates the dragons to monsters of the present

without writing a word about these days, about the vast glowering and mindless creature that moves in on Man at Man's bidding, in time of peace and reconstruction, to deliver him from labor, devours the earth, though it comes at first only when Man allows or calls. Man is eased of his burden, impressed by the size, the work that this force can perform. Although the work began when Man assembled this force, the Machine passes beyond Man's recall, replacing the old forms of living with the new. Human actions are now conditioned by the Machine. Things are not done, because the Machines don't like them. Demolition of the past comes easy with the power of this assembled force. Out of the dust of the ruins a modern Sauron, who begins as a Man and becomes a Board of Conrol, can conjure up visions of Man's future where there is no bloody sweat, no tears; all will be accomplished for Man's appetite with the lift of a finger, the blink of an eye, but at the cost of the deliverance of his future to the Board, computer-oriented Board, clean and shining Board, powerful beyond-all-the-measures-of-ordinary-Man Board. If Sauron has his way, there will be only one Board, and it's mustering, not in the shady lover of Mirkwood, but in carpeted, unbugged or bugged conference rooms, the gleaming glass walls of which look out over the City, down on the World. All that is required of Man is that he deliver his Fate into this calculation in return for a Machine-turned future comfort, and that he keep in cadence with the beat of the program devised and analyzed by some of the shine and some of the dark in his nature—that is all. The very creation of Man as a part of Nature is computed to a pattern that will permit a programmed development of the earth and beyond, by the Board.

Man's very seed will be tapped, analyzed and bottled for the correct ingredients needed for this time or that before it will be permitted to fertilize. Abortion will replace the Blessed Event, Euthanasia the Consolation. Environmental patterns, devised by programmers, correlated with words and sounds, will make poetry, music to dance to, in patterns better than any created by Man in the days when he danced for joy, for birth, for resurrection. The cruel punishment meted out to Prometheus, the fall of the son of Daedalus, the fell project of Pygmalion, all will be seen as mere fantasy, fit subjects for comedy. A fair lady to love will be made by a Higgins out of raw human stuff, not as a satire, but as a process to be lauded. There will be a musical comedy on the Crucifixion, as there are already flesh peddlers of the Old Testament.

Tolkien regards this future somberly; he sees it coming, which is why he is a conservative. Conservatives are disliked not for the right reasons, political, but for the wrong reasons, moral. Tolkien is sharp, and the bite in his writing shows how sharp he can be. When a fellow Oxford don exulted that now Oxford city was becoming alive, relating to progress, the High blocked and fumed with the traffic of Machines, Tolkien asked him how much more alive these cars were than the horse-drawn vehicles that had preceded them. And for most men, cars are more alive than living things. They polish them more than they ever curried horses, feed, scent and sink into them, make fancy women out of them, and killers, too.

Yet Tolkien is no dreamer with straw in his hair, no Endymion wandering around the Sacred Town babbling of brooks where once the wild thyme grew that now are muddied and greased over. Essentially he is a man of the traditional way, an apostle of rather addled common sense who sees Man for what he is and longs for him to put forth in all his staggering and vaulting majesty as the Son of God.

This yearning of Man to relate completely goes back to infancy and prenatal existence. The womb is the haven, flinching from the challenge life throws. Many a Man wants to return to it, and all Nature can be Mother. To be one with Nature and be Man too is unnatural, however much desired when the going gets tough, and the times call for sons of bitches. It is just as unnatural for Man to find a solution to his problems by handing himself over to the care of wise, Welfare-State Saruman, on the Board, who will curdle when he is not obeyed, or to Board member Sauron, who calls on the worst in Man, the nearest the surface and the most responsive, wherein lies the greatest danger of all: final self-destruction. Gandalf therefore is Tolkien's happiest subcreation, for, much against his will, many times, Gandalf backs away from taking over Man's fate, from joining the Board; instead, he poses the eternal dilemma, like Dante to the dreamer on the brim of Hell. He merely offers testimony and advice, shows the way on his great horse Shadowfax—a horse, to show how Tolkien can write,

> that might have been foaled in the morning of the world. The horses of the Nine cannot vie with him, tireless, swift as the flowing wind. . . . By day his coat glistens like silver; and by night it is like a shade, and he passes unseen. Light is his footfall! Never before had any man mounted him, but I took and tamed him. . . .

Gandalf still talks sense as a wisp of a wizard, foot-sore, old and gray, or shining with his white sort of wisdom. Gandalf knew the unique make-up of Man, he was one himself, in a way, as was Saruman his master and Sauron the evil one of the Gabala, but his shrewdness and learning made wisdom in him, argued him into love—in many ways the only sort of love is that arrived at through the mind's cognition—whereas the romantic nature of his master desired Man's soul for a diadem and Sauron wanted it as the industrial diamond that would permit his gyrating of the world.

Tolkien, through his Trilogy, shows the great value that all Nature and supernature sets upon Man. All, save Man himself, know Man's great value and worth. Poor Faust found out the real price, as did Dan'l Webster, in Stephen Benét's great tale. The Devil would give almost anything, save his own soul, to deny salvation, to get Man into his hands, and the comic irony is that Man will go to the Devil for the treading of a chick, for some tenderloin time, not knowing the price that he commands.

Man, in his womb-like yearning for a haven always closed, which has served only to launch him not to anchor, seeks ever for a warmth and light that Tolkien shows is not in this world; it cannot be given by other parts of Nature and can only be fleetingly revealed, as a token of what is to come. Tolkien is Tolkien. Kinfolk die and are part of it. Their way in life is the only guide to their final destination. The Cosmos is involved in Man and in his struggle to get beyond his body or stay with it. Occasionally Man sees a light; some are gifted to see over the wall into Death's world before they die and to pass back the news. Now and then Man thinks all things are visible and tangible and grasps at it all, falling through an error that often was a generous and loving search into another pitfall of Evil, waving a panacea as he falls.

The exaltation of all Nature and the Universe has been the theme of the Jesuit priest and scientist, Teilhard de Chardin. His writing has exercised an attraction both within and without his Church for those seeking an answer and a solace denied them by more traditional and orthodox theological writing. It has aroused grave suspicion and caveats from Authority, thereby undoubtedly increasing its attraction. And his theology is attractive and desirable, for it responds to modern Man's dilemma. It cushions the Cross, almost substituting a mindless Joy for Love, and makes One with Nature. His theme is the very opposite of Tolkien's, which above all is traditional, stern and unrelenting in its vigorous portrayal of Man as a being born for trouble as surely as sparks fly upward. But, as with C.S. Lewis and Charles Williams, readers sense a likeness between Teilhard de Chardin and Tolkien, and they are wrong again. Teilhard, that dubious Jesuit, hymns the Universe:

Always from the very first it was the world, greater than all the elements which make up the world, that I was in love with, and never before was there anyone before whom I could in honesty bow down.

His lyrical book of devotion, *The Divine Milieu*, like hot cakes grasped and devoured by the spiritually hungry, fearful and insecure, is dedicated "For those who love the world."

This is altogether at odds with the unromantic, unblinking philosophy that Jacques Maritain has distilled from the Greek and the Latin, from his own creed, which fits Tolkien's Trilogy as a sword its scabbard.

Lewis, Williams and their kind, even Teilhard de Chardin, have more in common with Chesterton than ever Tolkien had, although he shared the same Church as G.K.C. There is something basically jolly about Chesterton, and Lewis and his like needed it, mirrored it, so as to whistle past the graveyard. Charles Williams always had in mind that happy land beyond his life. He saw Heaven through the wonders he conjured up on earth.

Never does Tolkien relent in all the sweep of his story into anything romantic or joyful—there is only jollity in the Hobbits—for he realizes that Chestertonian light and cheer are phantasmagoria, and that the Truth, rough and bitter as it may be, can afford the only real solace, the only real aid to Man in his trouble. Chesterton saw this too, as he fleetingly shows here and there in *The Ballad of the White Horse*, but, a journalist as well as a genius, he had to produce for editors and public, so he served up prose and poetry as if it were foaming brown ale and swallowed his own bitter brew behind the bar. All other relations, save the one that Tolkien delivers, fail at the edge of the grave, although they dance at weddings. Once Tolkien's message—no new one, but the old belief that Man dislikes and in the end rejects—is realized, it is not too hard to bear, even cherish; Man has his dignity. But neither is it easy, although it has its own sardonic humor, a soldier's kind. It is because Tolkien only reaffirms, so beguilingly and exhilaratingly, the old tenet of his race that he insists this work is that of subcreation, not creation. Were Tolkien's tenet of his own creation, as Teilhard de Chardin's message is of his, it would be diminished in significance, a new and fledgling belief, not an ancient-rooted truth revealed again for this time and age.

Tolkien accomplishes this in his tale of this relation so vigorously and gives such enjoyment to the reader with his legendary story of it that, because his story is heard even when it is read, the words sound like an organ in full bellow, working through a light voluntary air to the entire majesty of a symphony, with the grave calm and measured consolation of a recessional.

The entire action of the Trilogy is vivid and continued. The words run ahead of the tale as if they were running footmen bearing burning links into the growing dark of the story. The great art of Story is to tell the reader what is happening not only on the surface, but below and above also and, above all, what is to come, what may be ahead around the turn of a page. Every ploy of literary merit Tolkien can handle he uses to enthrall the reader. The great size of the book needs a heroic resolve even to start, so Tolkien makes it easy, thereby losing some readers but gaining many more, by his Hobbit larking. Possibly Tolkien could never have carried it through but for his domestic stability, any more than he can finish the fourth part of it, the addendum, *The Silmarillion*, without it, despite learning, craft, listeners and friends, and most of them are new, as the old pass on and he grows old. Moreover, he could never have conceived it alone had he not seen the collapsing of his world, built on his ancient premises.

Tolkien could no more blink this heroic theme, once he had taken up his pen to the task of it, than falter in his creed, and that's been tried and tested. In the end *The Hobbit* turned out to be not for children, as he had meant to be, but the hook of his own device that pulled him into the deep of *The Lord of the Rings*. The great theme of his work he found before him majestically expressed in the words of old that came before his English and produced it. He Englished the beat of the Norse. Courage and its exercise are the only reward, the prosecution of courage that may give a bit more time of light before the dark comes down again, maybe forever. Man is called to the side of Good in his tales, not by a promise of victory, not for a reward in the Hereafter, whatever that may be, but because that is Man's reason for being, to go down battling for the idea of Man, the only piece of Creation not bound by the forces of Nature alone. Time and time again he gives his people and their company a chance to cop out, but with every decision to go on they become stronger in resolution as the strength of their bodies drains. They enrage the corps of the Evil Host of Sauron. Good is seen as a positive, and the use of it, like the use of love, only makes it stronger, as the neglect of it makes it harder to come by. One great advantage unknown to Frodo and his fellowship is that they can see something of the other side, they can understand something of Evil, having tasted it and enjoyed the taint and taste of corruption, furtively, guiltily—as who has not? But the Enemy cannot see their side, cannot conceive what it is to be good. The Enemy has lost the Good, forever: this is a part of their corruption that works against Sauron and his ilk and saves the wretch Gollum for a time, for he still remembers furtively the Good. It is a blessing little realized: that the Bad always underestimate the

Good. This works most of the time, too, but mostly in the End, when the Bad put on the pressure.

Friends can be as welcome as good news. It is better to be befriended than to be rich or blooming. Tolkien is conscious of this; it runs all through is tale. From their homes in the Shire he calls his Hobbits, from their warm beds and loving arms—more than that for faithful Sam and more to come for Merry and for Pippin. Friendship is the protection that cannot be bought with anything but the giving of it. Chaos, greed and unreason may win every daily round, the Good may lose, even forever. But for all that, there is an exultant belief that defeat is no reason even to consider surrender when there are still friends. Tolkien, from the well of his learning, from his knowledge of the Norse, fashions a story that honors Man by throwing away the carrot, showing Man he is no donkey, but a lord, able to make his own way even if it ends up in the knacker's yard, able to struggle to death against the rest of the world to the very end—to an end worth fighting for. This is Tolkien's great contribution to those who read his Trilogy. The Ring, the final one, is a terrible instrument of Evil. The struggle for its destruction is the lot of Man, a purpose more worthy than all the promises of carrots, pies in the sky. These are bribes, often well-intended, fit for children and those who grow up only to be old, for those weakened by adversity and environment. These the dying will not forgive, when they need true consolation, realizing that they have been propped through days with lies. Only the Truth brings real compassion and dignity to die with; it cannot be denied.

There is in Tolkien, as there was in the beginning of his kind of Story, in the lands of the North, long before Christ hit them, always good company. That is what Man now lacks, save in primitive societies such as in the Aran Isles. Man does not know it, for he is gelded of it by the world and given sex instead. If there is no friendship, only sex, there is no marriage, only a temporary convenience that should not be bound in sacramental ties. A vow cannot be broken: habit can. And concupiscence, pleasant and devouring as it can be, is the reverse of a contract, because promises are made to be kept, and so is marriage, for better or for worse: there's the nub and rub of it. The lesson of Narcissus is lost: he has become just a pretty boy who looked at himself. Men need their own company, need to match their minds, like minds. C.S. Lewis waxed lyrical over it: "No sound delights me more than Man's laughter." And in his preface to *Essays Presented to Charles Williams* he is brimming with a wholly natural affection for men such as Williams. And, embarrassing as this might be, Lewis had a point that is lost in this Mom society.

The Inklings found pleasure in their own company. It guarded them and made them ready, through their reading and writing and the conclusions drawn from them, facing thereby some of the blows of their fates that would have finished them had they been alone. And they were all smitten; no Ivory Tower is Oxford, any more than any other place.

The best way one of Tolkien's creations can act is to be a Man. Don Tolkien defends the dignity of being human. The Victorians made do with the antics of animals dressed up in dolls' clothing, speaking quaintly in human kind—there is a touch of this in *The Hobbit*—before Tolkien came into his prime. The older fantasies cheered men with falsehood and heresies, lulled them with dreams of their own thumb-sucking thinking, until Tolkien revealed a harder, sterner, yet more ancient truth that Man can bear, once he gets the gist of it.

Tolkien will shift uneasily from this version of his motive. The last man to ask motive of is an artist, always; it's not even fair. The interpretation given to his work in one report, following an interview and some accounts of hipster gatherings, where Tolkien's characters, Gandalf and Frodo especially, had been raised on high, in Golden Gate Park in San Francisco and in student sit-ins in the University of Chicago, gives a psychedelic twist, a long-haired, uncombed look to his work. "More than a campus craze, it's like a drug dream," the *New York Times* had it, and the Hobbits are pinned to print as inventions of a bored Oxford don, as a benevolent, furry-footed, half-pint people "who have taken the rising generation by storm."

Magic in Tolkien is never mumbo-jumbo, kid stuff, a knotted-sheet rope for escape artists. When the earth heaves open or the sky cleaves, Heaven or Hell may be breaking through. Heaven is not to be hoped for as coming

71

here, it is not even realized, only sensed as what comes after. When Bilbo and Frodo sailed away to the Grey Havens, in the gentle rain there came a fragrance of sweet flowers, the sound of singing over the water. There, as in a dream, not in this world, Frodo saw the curtain of the rain rolled back and white shores rise bordering a faraway country of green, Hy-Brasil of Erin, maybe, and the sun came up, the sun that was the old glory, not just a ball of molten mass, a source of nuclear power.

CHAPTER VIII

THE ONCE AND THE FUTURE

Behind the loneliness and hostility of this world there is throughout the Universe—Tolkien writes what he knows —waiting to be freed and seen, a real sense of communion that runs and merges all ages into one. But this union centers around Man: Man is more than part of it; it is his. This communion is the opposite of alienation. The antithesis of one big union, it is, rather, a correlation to a pattern. It requires action and courage to correlate, not just to get back into the bed with Nature. It is given only to some, with many a backward glance, as to the Fellowship of the Ring, to go out beyond Nature, whence is Man's future, if he is to have one. Bilbo led in his small way and Frodo in his great one, along with Strider, whom he made a King, the King of Man's desiring. Strider's coronation came from Frodo's efforts above all, which is why the Hobbit is Everyman, as all men are, shaken from his Shire and little ways.

The working out of this theme in Tolkien's mind and then in his words makes *The Hobbit* the genesis of *The Lord of the Rings*, no mere doodle. To understand that Trilogy deep down without at length reading the earlier book is to read *The Once and Future King* by T.H. White while ignoring his *The Sword in the Stone*. It can be done, and may be better done; that way makes for easier reading, for a quick solution. It is easy to follow, the big before the little, but the earlier, simple book serves as a solution at the end.

The Arthurian tale of T.H. White possesses some of the same quality as *The Lord of the Rings* and, like the Tolkien, is too little regarded, for all its popularity. Like Tolkien's Trilogy it reveal the irrevocable reaction that comes from those willing enough to face the results of their decision: Arthur above all realizes that both to enjoy and to honor justice and equality, not just for knights, but for knaves, not just for the rich and tubbed, but for the poor and dirty, for those one cannot like and yet by the acceptance of their code are bound to love, the King and his court must be bound by the rule of it also. So Lance and Jenny have to flee, and he too must bear the burden of his sins. Few knights were able to stand up to this reeling implication, and the hoods took over.

Once the sacramental bread was broken at the Round Table—better than Lewis or Williams is White on the religious theme—it behooved those who there broke their fast, who yearned to sip from the Grail before they died of the Quest for it, that they share that bread and wine with all, hereby losing and, worse, denying all their privileges and titles, all for a crust of bread and sip of wine from a battered cup. But the cup contained their God, who could only be drunk so. Few think it worth the trouble.

The Arthurian rule was far harder than chivalry, and the knights of Arthur did not grasp it all. But there it was, and they followed it or fell away. Physical love, too, has an end, in this book, as in life. The marriage bond is broken there, and sin sets in. Sadness is there at the end; Carnaby Street-clad goons take over from the older, plumed knights. Yet the tale, vulgarized, bowdlerized on stage and screen as *Camelot*, made the butt of sick jokes since Kennedy, deserves Tolkien's respect. It will please the reader, any reader worth the name. It is claptrap to think White was writing for children, or writing for the birds, falconer that he was. Writing for Man is the only way, even for children to read, and T.H. White writes this way. He was a man full of lore, too. He and Tolkien were birds of a feather, although they would have made a strange pair together. They did not write *The Hobbit* and

The Sword in the Stone just for nothing, for children, although they thought they did and it might seem that way, any more than Lewis Carroll wrote for Alice, any more than the first antic strides of a new Marine are meant primarily to make the young laugh, although they may, and it is good that they should. Those strides may lead the lad to death in a paddy field, to his moment of truth, as writing did White.

Tolkien came to his realization of *The Lord of the Rings* almost reluctantly. Certainly he has never been clear about it, embarrassed maybe, like that strawboot recruit Marine. He is as evasive of questions about his writing as a Hobbit, as he is of questions about human relations generally, for the same sort of reason: Frodo could be Tolkien's middle name. He insists that he would rather have written the books in Elvish, so there: put that in a pipe and smoke it. In a lengthy, erudite and difficult appendix he explains that the Elvish tongues are of the west-elves (The Elder), of the Eldarin form. Two of these tongues appear, the High-Elven (Quenya) and the Grey-Elven (Sindarin).

An artist should never apologize, never explain. Dialectic is not in an artist, or he would not be one; he'd be a dialectician, a very different kind of person. But Tolkien doggedly goes on with his appendix; it entrances him, thought it would be better set away from the story. Sindarin was the tongue of daily use, and Quenya was the ceremonial tongue, used for ritual, lore and song, and so on, and on, and on. This is the sort of footnote that has further irritated and misled critics such as Edmund Wilson and Philip Toynbee, neither of whom could stand the style and story anyhow. Critics know by this time that the author's account of a story is the least relevant. Who ever has heard of a good exegesis by the creator of any piece of art? An author does not even know what he looks like, walks like, sounds like; he knows only about his work, he cannot talk about that, for it's his rebirth, and, outside the Rabelaisian nonsense, to talk about that is beyond even creative artists, as artists. Yet Tolkien and others like him are excoriated for their halting, lame, impatient, different, erudite, expiatory or defiant explanations of their acts of creation. It is asking of Life: How?

Tolkien, in one defense, says that *The Lord of the Rings* began as a philological fun game:

> The invention of languages is the foundation. The "stories" were made rather to provide a world for these languages than the reverse. . . . It is to me, anyway, largely an essay in "linguistic esthetic", as I sometimes say to people who ask me "what is it all about?" . . . Certainly it has no allegorical intentions, general, particular or topical, moral, religious or political.

That is just nonsense, and serve them right who believe it, if any really do.

His own description of the genesis of his short story *Leaf by Niggle* refutes this denial of allegory. The only time a writer can explain is by telling another story: Evelyn Waugh did it in *The Ordeal of Gilbert Pinfold*, Edna O'Brien has done it often, so have Doris Lessing, Anthony Powell, Joyce. In fact, there is a lot of Niggle in Tolkien himself. Niggle, a painter, was not too successful because he had so many other things to do, and did them reasonably well, and because his kind heart was the sort that made him uncomfortable if he did nothing about things he cared about and felt he should do something about. When he did anything that he should have, he was apt to grumble about it, lose his temper, mutter and swear (mostly to himself). All of this is very like Tolkien. As Niggle helped his neighbor sometimes and people from afar off, so did he—Tolkien's kindness to his students through the years shows through their work. People kept Niggle away from his pictures, which were too large and ambitious for his skill anyway, as are all themes of all artists: the artist satisfied is worse than dead. Niggle longed to paint trees, when all he could paint very well was the sheen of a single leaf. (The Leaf is *The Hobbit,* the Tree the Trilogy.) All Niggle ever really accomplished was the painting of a leaf—Tolkien wrote the story in 1939, before *The Lord of the Rings* could have seemed possible to him in all its length, breadth and strength—and that painting was destroyed when the Town Museum burned down, as Time fires up everything, sooner or later. Yet Niggle's name will be remembered because his actions kept his memory green, and a place of rest and healing was called after him. There is already a Tolkien Tower for many men, and Lothlórien is their desired place of rest.

Tolkien came to write that Niggle story, he says, because of a relationship that grew between him and a tree, the branches and foliage of which he could see from his bed when he was young, living in Sarehole. When the tree was cut down, nobody remembered it, it seemed to Tolkien, save himself, so the story is in memory of that long-gone tree. That is all he has to say about the story; it makes sense: more power to him.

Father Giles of Ham, a smaller version of the dominant theme of his greater subcreation, is more easy for the young to hear than either *The Hobbit* or the Trilogy. It partakes of the same structure, and courage breaks through to aid the small hero and sustain him through the perils cast by giants and by dragons. It lisps a little, stumbles like Strawboot, a recruit of a book, a lesson in arms for Tolkien.

The Adventures of Tom Bombadil are verses from the Red Book of Westmarch, the book of Hobbit lore, and they can be tiresome to read, though there are illuminating snatches. It is Tolkien at his worst, yet its exuberance is a redeeming feature for those who have the tolerance. The verses that festoon the Trilogy in songs and incantations are a part of Tolkien's pride. They must be permitted him, and, though they fail to attain the high level of the reality of that subcreation, they do make Tolkien clearer.

Very different by far, verging too much on scholarship and translation to be any more popular than a translation of the *Battle of Maldon, The Dream of the Road* or *Sir Gawaine and the Green Knight* is Tolkien's version of *The Homecoming of Beorhtnoth, Beorhthelm's Son*. It has the sense and beat of *Beowulf*. Here is Tolkien at his scholarly subcreative best—the Art of Translation—writing for other scholars and students of the English tongue; general readers are not in his mind. This poem helps to explain why the seemingly dull discipline of philology is so attractive to those who break through the moldy crust that covers it because of the wretched teaching of the subject by grammarians.

Most of the readers of *The Hobbit* care not that even the pronunciation of the name of this work is beyond them. It is an exhilarating experience to hear Tolkien read Anglo-Saxon, Norse and his Elvish; the cadence and the message of his subcreation run clear and strong. The ancient expression of heroic will, lofted aloud in *Beowulf*, is found in *The Homecoming*, spoken in a dream of Tohrthelm. In Tolkien's version:

Will shall be the sterner, heart the bolder, spirit the greater as our strength lessens.

There is Tolkien's theme: his life and work are based on it. And if obstinacy, irritability, a sour conservatism take over the man now and then, those are honorable wounds. After his years in the field, indeed, it seems but luck that he remains so hale.

No writer is ever understood as he expects to be, unless he writes a technical manual, and that will last only a little while. Thus his *Homecoming* is not a book so much as a matter of fact in the form of one. Tolkien's work has to be judged by the reader; it's up to him what he makes of it, as of any work of art. Some people see their own mother in a Gauguin and are moved; others may see there the degradation of the Lotus and are moved too. Rembrandt's great painting of the "Two Negroes," in The Hague, has a meaning that changes even with the times. It is no wonder Tolkien wrote (February 2, 1967): "I dislike being written about and the results to date have caused me both irritation and distaste"; for, of all popular writers, Tolkien is out of step with these times. There, perhaps, is the reason for his popularity among the young: they are out of step too; they are listening for the beat of the drum, the distant drum that their old Gandalf hears.

In a second edition of *The Hobbit* Tolkien wrote that he hoped to proceed with a background of "history of Elvish tongues." Perhaps he said it to cover his tracks, to calm the Inklings who were having about all they could take of his Hobbits. What he accomplished was more rewarding for the world, even if it did not satisfy him. He should leave well enough alone: what he has written, how it comes out. No revised editions! There should be a law about it: no second thoughts, revised editions, for creative writing! There are some writers, some artists in all fields, who cannot leave well enough alone after their creation is born. Rouault was like that, always calling his paintings home for retouching, repainting even. He burned hundreds of them because he did not care for them, sending his agent foaming, gibbering into Law against him. Evelyn Waugh's revised edition of *Brideshead Revisited* is not as good as the first, not because of the differences—who can find them?—but because of the uneasy feeling engendered in the reader that maybe Waugh's conscience was bothering him and was trying to get him into the divorce and abortion arguments of Waugh's Church. Every time Frank O'Connor had the opportunity, for anthologies, second editions, he would revise his stories. It's wrong; there should be a law against it.

Tolkien was driven to the sequel of *The Hobbit*, was impelled to write *The Lord of the Rings* the way it is, whether he knew it or not. The tale grew in the telling, taking more than ten years, interspersed with his academic duties, scholarly pursuits, his family and World War II, during which decade Tolkien moved from house to house, from College to College (Exeter to Merton), from Chair to Chair (Philology to English Literature). And though all his moves were within a stone's throw of Tom Tower, yet they were as disturbing to him as it is to a proper Hobbit to move abode, to break step with the old tried and trusted order. When the story was completed, in longhand, it had to be revised and rewritten backward, naturally—how else? Then the three volumes were typed and retyped by himself, for he was unable to afford the expense of a professional typist.

In addition, Tolkien was overwhelmed with trying to answer his correspondence without the help of a secretary. Later, when he had one, he was still overwhelmed, for he could no more use a secretary than a working man a valet or a costermonger a butler. The correspondence has been snowballing since the first publication of *The Lord of the Rings*. It comes as a surprise to learn how much men such as Lewis and Tolkien feel impelled to accept and answer all their mail. Any public man, and Tolkien is one, whether he likes it or not, needs the filter of an agent, a secretary he can trust. To use energy designed and geared for subcreation to slit envelopes, to file correspondence, to read crank mail, begging letters from professionals, lay, secular and crook, disperses it. Lewis' recently collected letters, edited by his brother, show the result of this.

The hurly-burly of the Trilogy's popularity, which surprised him greatly, has blurted this truth out of him: "The prime motive was the desire of a tale-teller to try his hand at a really long story that would hold the attention of the readers, delight them, and at times maybe excite them or deeply move them." That is about it; the rest follows.

He is refreshingly burly and truculent—a feature of Tolkien—about those among the many readers who have read it, or at least reviewed it, and have found it "boring, absurd or contemptible," saying that he has "no cause to complain since I have similar opinions of their works, or of the kinds of writing that they evidently prefer." He made the same sort of crack about the critics in his *Beowulf* lecture, in 1936.

When he says that there is no inner meaning or "message" in his work, that to provide one was not his intention, he hedges. He does agree that any history, feigned or true, will react upon the individual reader, each with his own varied background and experience. And yet this is all that there ever is of message, all that any good writer can attempt. The reader is free to make what he can or what he likes of the author's presentation, as he is of the dream in which Dante took him to the edge of Hell.

If there is more than that, the author claims a domination, and Tolkien knows that such assertiveness is deadly to Art, kills it, renders it down to a mere instrument of propaganda. There is nothing in the book that is directly related to any present experience or to the history of the world around us; the reader must interpret all such relations. Some do, some don't.

For all that, war cast its shadow over Tolkien; he was a Fusilier, and "one has indeed personally to come under the shadow of war to feel its oppression. . . . By 1918 all but one of my close friends were dead." This is true, as far as it goes. Moreover, he had an eye for country; he loved to walk over England, through the woods, over the hills that miraculously, even today, remain clear and quiet. There is an emptiness about the Highlands of Scotland; Hugh MacLennan points out that they have the same sense of space as Canada affords. Many times Owen Barfield, among others, recalls the long days of walking that can be such a delight; Tolkien was in the company he speaks of. Long before *The Lord of the Rings* was written, there are accounts of Tolkien's fellowship, coming upon a welcome inn or farm as the dark is falling, of the warm and the talk around the fire within a circle of trees, far from any sounds of the city or examination mills.

The geography of the Trilogy is important only in the fact that it has to be understood, the way Tolkien describes it, to let the action develop. There are places of pastoral countryside still in England. There are moors, windswept and lonely, Tolkien knows, in Devon, Cornwall Northumberland. The forests of Middle-earth still survive in the Forest of Dean. The mountains of his tale must have arisen in his inward eye from Snowden with its snowcap, seen from Holyhead, from where the ships go westward to a strange green land, where there is a strange sort of peace and living not of this world. The caverns of his tale are all over Britain. The place is riddled with them; not a week goes by without their making the news with some disaster or derring-do down in them.

This Middle-earth, this realm of his imagination that became a more-than-national heritage, is peopled with men and women of high degree, wizards, elves, dwarves, monsters of all kinds, as well as Hobbits, who stand between the others and Man as his relation. It is a world that has much in common with the land of Morte d'Arthur and other tales of Faery.

There is something deeper even than can be found in the Arthurian Cycle that T.H. White used to such advantage in *The Once and Future King*. The acclaim that has compared Tolkien to Malory and Spenser, and preferred him to Ariosto, meted out by reputable like-thinking scholars and critics, not by others, fails to realize Tolkien's contribution. He is not to be compared with the writers of the past. Tolkien is a *non-pareil*. He does not follow in an orderly, literary, evolutionary development. He lacks the lightness and the elegance of Spenser. He goes back to the source; subcreating is his word for it, and it gets less clumsy to use as his work becomes clearer. His style raises the hackles of Edmund Wilson, who swipes so fast and hard at the Tolkien subcreation, the Hobbits, which his own child loves so much, and at *The Lord of the Rings,* believing that it is but kid stuff, a philological bill of goods. Tolkien's lightness with his profound scholarship comes hard to Wilson, who reveres and proclaims his own self-taught erudition.

There is always something truculent about those who sit about defeating the scholars at their own craft, and yet, somehow, it cannot be done. They can be caught out in particulars, in their general appreciation even, they can be correlated and their learning set in a new perspective that they failed to realize, but they cannot be replaced. Theirs is the only way to learning, as accretive and abrasive often as a coral reef. Thus there is something of Coulton, that "remote and ineffectual don" who added up the Middle Ages, in Tolkien.

There are grounds for supposing that it might all be a game, *The Hobbit,* Trilogy and all. Tolkien plants the seed of that suspicion himself. It might well have been, Tolkien claims, just an exercise, an experiment that turned out remarkably well. The work got beyond him certainly, led him perhaps unwillingly, with his beliefs, into the public forum. Popularity, especially when it is of the extent and variety that has come to Tolkien, contains elements of malignity: it has soured Tolkien, ruined lesser men. The philological abstraction is so minutely and delicately set in his subcreation of a world wherein the Hobbits, the beloved creatures of his imagination, play such a role as has never before been conceived for Halflings, for little people, that they assume, in time of crisis, a dignity and a heroism that seem infused in them from a supernatural source; they are delivered into a state of Grace. They are the medium for his philosophy. Only before the action and when, after it is over, they revert and return to their natural state in the Shire, do they engage the mind of the reader with their furry feet and comfort-loving ways, their quaintly rustic or schoolboy jargon of Tolkien's youth. Yet just before they return, letting their weapons show and their arms flex ready for action, they are prepared to set about some roughs and seem to welcome the idea of trouncing them, killing them maybe, if they ask for trouble. They do this as Hobbits, Merry, Pippin and Sam, and Tolkien does not pursue this event, but it occurs after they

81

have reached their state of Grace; their reactions to man's ruffianism are a new side to their nature that has implications uneasy to contemplate. Their return to the happy days to come, to the days of old, is what Tolkien intended, and he can deny, to save embarrassment or involvment, that there was any change wrought in them by the encounter with the Ring, where they saved Man. Tolkien blames the reader, for using his own thoughts.

There is a reality in the Trilogy, which does not appear in *The Hobbit*, that is transcendent, that goes far beyond realism, as painters, composers and sculptors do, to express more profoundly the truth that lies hidden behind realism, and it takes some getting used to. The visual arts have broken through to this, but generally the written arts have failed.

Tolkien's apprehension—above all the Trilogy is an apprehensive tale—goes far beyond dragons or the machine monsters of today. The most important element in the Norse myth lies in Courage, and Tolkien comes back to that time and time again. This is the great contribution of the sagas of the North to Man's delivery: not the courage of the brute, of the wolverine, not the theory of courage spelled out by either chivalry or strategy, but, above all, courage that does not count on victory or even expect it. Courage is the end in itself, the goal of Man.

There is an exultant titanic aura surrounding the battling of the gods of the Norse that is wholly lacking in the bolt-throwing Olympians, the deities who become the darlings of men in the flesh, who couple with swans, like bulls, as well as in human kind, interfere for their sons and lovers below, often using tricks and other unnatural means of intervention. The Olympians always win, if their men do not, but with the Norse the winner can be the Enemy. Chaos can come again and again and put them down, but this is no reason for surrender either to them or to men fit to be in their company, men strong enough, cast in such heroic temper to realize that only in abiding resistance to the Enemy, Evil, who has won a lasting sally point even within their very minds, ages and appetites, is there the reason for their pride.

This great lesson of the sagas predates Christianity, and it is a perfect lesson because it is void of promise or of demeaning reward. It is realistic, too; for all men are not equal to the challenge, are not born so, can never become so. The poor, the weak, the wrong will always be with Man and in him, debilitating, pulling him down. They are a part of the human condition, and if this is realized out of Tolkien, the reader will have won in the face of this world, where all the powers are leagued to deny this cardinal truth, either because they are romantic or because they are evil. It is without hope, save for that of his own condition and making, that Man must struggle to be worth his being.

Flashes of genius showed through the froth of G.K. Chesterton, bewildering by their lightning, as in his *Ballad of the White Horse*, where the only comfort vouchsafed to Saxon Alfred by the Mother he conjures up is that the night grows darker yet and the seas rise higher, that Heaven is but an iron cape, that there is no cause in joy nor any hope in faith. Faith, like all virtues, is hard to come by, hard to keep. Slippered ease is retreat, the playing of a harp, obeisance and ritual, but time off for wounds' recovery.

Tolkien's Trilogy is no elvish *summa*, no primitive pagan allegory as some of his admirers hope, no inspired nonsense of jabberwocks in a tulgy wood, but the relation only possibly realized in words by a scholar who is possessed of Faith in Man, sees pie in the sky as ludicrous and as childish as pie in the face or firmament good enough to eat. Tolkien uses his learning, wisdom and lore to project out of largely old and well-known literary fact and legend a revelation so complete that it is a new and refreshing literary subcreation that is unique.

There is Revelation everywhere in Tolkien, a myriad of details, comic, tragic and work-a-day, that are apart from his main theme, different in level, presentation and degree, yet all combining into a variegated whole of many hues and styles.

The more knowledge possessed of Tolkien and his literary work, the more does the power of his subcreation grow. A man cannot be divorced from his writing, however much he may desire to be. His own relation tends to obscure, to be dismissed anyhow, and the interpretations developed by critics tend to be even more misguiding and are many times malicious. Yet the facts will out: they are essential for the understanding of the work. And the more a writer can find it in him to reveal about the facts of his being, the better it generally is. It will bay the critics, even if it does send them snuffling around family trees.

Tolkien's work, like all Art, demands attention, intellectual effort, if it is to be known; this is what Art is. After the first shock or pleasure of relation it can only respond, not generate anymore. There must be will, however unrealized by the reader, viewer, listener: he must participate. So does he become a subcreator himself, bringing new life to the word "art" by his own vision and interpretation of it.

The whole significance that Tolkien has presented comes from his background and belief; it emanated from him although he wrote it as it was of place and time other than Oxford, England, of these days. The world of history and geography, of strange tongues and wondrous happenings, his Middle-earth, the Third Age, is but the place of his literary incarnation, where he conveniently and with less embarrassment gives flesh to his Word. Besides, people may read it if it does not get too near the bone of their present dilemma. Fantasy has this great quality: it can reveal the apprehension, beliefs and even joy to be had in the present by casting the tale of these times in a form that seems so charming and archaic that it appears at first as if it is a babble of green fields under a timeless sky in Faraway, where the reader can roam as freely as a child. So he can, and return there as often as he reads again such a book as *The Lord of the Rings*. But through the eyes of that child he sees the present world and his place in it, so that while the pleasure of his visit to Faraway remains, it is the necessary mirror also for him of his days on this earth and his place in them.

Tolkien's words go far beyond the Happening of the Trilogy. There is a delicate balance that keeps the razor-thin edge of his message from being nicked, blunted or destroyed, safe from critics even. The myriad details of his relation do not crowd out the sum of his relation. This is a considerable feat, when the multiplicity of action and ideas that he presents is realized. There is rarely a page in the Trilogy that does not contain an action or a happening of its own.

CHAPTER IX

AS IT WAS AND WILL BE

Tolkien's Hobbit was a creature he chose with care, one small enough to look up to Man's image of himself, one small enough for Man to look down on, one he could not submit to or let be bolder than himself. The Hobbit is Man's own daring admission of himself as he really is. Moreover, the nearer to the earth, as the Hobbit is, the more the earth possesses, the more the earth gives. Grounded on the earth, Frodo has lived below it. Strider and Gandalf, even the Ents, whose roots stretch deep, see farther, higher than the Hobbits, and so they miss much that lies about them. And the elves are too starry-eyed to care, the dwarves too jealous and full of their own concern. Gollum, called Smeagol in happier times, snuffled the earth and below only for his Precious, the Ring. The power of Evil, Sauron, too, knew the earth well. The Trolls and goblins were of it, knew what the earth could divulge. The Hobbit strolled, taking his ease on the earth, patted the ground, cultivated it for the good food that grows there, lifting his eyes from it only to see what the sky had in store for his land.

Man searches the sky for omens and signs, as he does even when he does not have to; when there is nothing on the horizon, Man's eyes will still search it for something that he does not even know or expect, but hopes for. It is his destiny. The fecund, feckless things of earth escape his vision, but never the view of the Hobbits; they see them all day long. It is in the revelation and far-seeing of heroic Strider and wise, good Gandalf that the way is set for action, but never is the tale too far off the ground, because the Hobbit marches, trots beside Man, is the link that draws Man to the earth that grew them, however long ago. Man is of the earth earthy, and of the Heaven too.

Man is of many degrees. The feudal concept that Tolkien proposes and accepts is out of step with these romantic, therefore evil, times, when all men are considered equal because they all deserve to be. The heroic legend, the history of Man, denies his equality, substituting an aristocracy for a democracy. Benvolence is regarded as a cardinal virtue; the very function of the strong is to protect the weak, and there are men strong and good in Tolkien's canon. They are men far removed from the general mass, who, though the ranks of the rare are open, so that men come and go through them, arise even from among the Hobbits to be leaders among them. There is an aristocracy of the few who contain among them the strength to lead the careless, unminding, limited many. It is among the many that the Enemy of the Fellowship finds his legions—Tolkien's good company are very few—and never until now has this concept of the chivalric leadership been so close to coming to a close since the many have chosen the Leader, or the Leader has destroyed the Fellowship. The only wonder is that Tolkien has not been even more vigorously attacked: Fantasy perhaps has saved him.

There is an interplay of plots, of action, that pleasantly distracts with bewildering fascination from the dour, overriding theme. The byplay, if read, offers creature antics, thrills and excitement, allows the reader to comprehend the high theme of the story—but only if he wants to. There's great fun in it anyway. He cannot help but know that something is going on below and around that is pretty serious, but there is an entire dear world of daily life, fantastic and charming, more exciting than *The Thirty-nine Steps*, and that can be enough. It must be, for most of the readers, although all must get a flicker of the fire below the yarn of adventure.

The Fellowship of the Ring, in trying to save peace on earth for Man and all beings of goodwill—that is the high enterprise of the work—finally offers itself as a sacrifice in battle to let Frodo carry the Ring to destruction.

The Hobbit always remains in the reader's mind, even through *The Lord of the Rings*. Among the Inklings it was referred to as the "new Hobbit book."

Tolkien called *The Hobbit* a children's book, not only because it was one in the beginning, but also because he wanted to avoid the sort of questions that inevitably arose about it as the years enveloped his work with significance and popularity. There was in *The Hobbit* the start of it all, and the start of action that leads on and on often is not even realized as significant at the very time it happens, the turn up one road and not another, the face seen in a ferry, just for a moment of time, the opening of a book in idle curiosity, the apparently casual encounters in which there often is the beginning of the action. It was Bilbo's challenge by Gandalf, the taunt of the dwarves in the beginning of *The Hobbit*, that started it all, as it turned out. Bilbo's response, haltingly expressed, began the Hobbit's sharing of the whole great theme. Tolkien, perhaps, fell into the pit that he had been digging for himself all his life, thinking it was just a burrow he was getting into.

Art has a life of its own, and each life has an art of its own too; it is discovering them both and making them one that makes the artist the necessary man. He establishes the communion, makes of it the sacrament. Every man makes his own version. Full communion rarely occurs, anywhere, anytime, and the full implications of where it will go or end are unknown, even to the artist—perhaps, finally, to him least of all.

This is more the case with Tolkien than he realizes; it is a quality shared by Proust and others. Proust, like Tolkien, is removed from most of his readers and admirers by a difference in belief, background and thought that is more impenetrable than a thorn hedge. James Joyce, on the other hand, is all there with the people who read him, once they get over his prose or see him as himself. Leo Bloom's a Hobbit with a Dublin accent and a downcast eye, without a Gandalf. Joyce writes out of a contempt, a rejection that he felt for people with whom he has nearly everything in common. Tolkien is quite the reverse, an academic conservative aristocrat.

The Trilogy is the stuff of the fairy tale, of myth and legend, of the folk tale that contains the matter of Man, far beyond what it seems to be. Tolkien brings our dragons home to roost. Orcs and Trolls, dwarves, elves and Ents surround us, only their guise is different. All the life in the Trilogy is related to Man; he makes sense of the lot of it.

Man clings to Life, thereby giving power to Death, because he hopes to get from Life what, for Man in particular, has been cruelly denied him. That is why Death is feared. The insecure and the poor, the unfulfilled, want Life to continue so that they may be around if there is relish. Death brings a finish to their hope, as if Death were the end, not just a manifestation of the seasons of the earth.

The great danger in any analysis, literary or scholarly, of Tolkien's work lies in the fragmentation that happens. This bothers Tolkien, who is impatient of any exegesis, denying the sense of it. Nowadays he denies many things that he should not. He knows the harm analysis can do. He revealed this in his British Association lecture on *Beowulf*. He pointed this out in one of the allegories that he despises: after a wholesale study of a belvedere, when it has been taken apart stone by stone and scattered for research by the critics, the maker of it returns and there is no place left for him to climb and to look out over the sea. Tolkien has screened his own motives for writing in order to repel the critics. He will not have them aboard his work if he can help it. He preserves his private vision doughtily and alone. Tolkien's subcreation cannot be taken to pieces; it is all of one piece with the man who made it. It will fall to pieces if it is pulled apart.

People who tend toward Tolkien because of their similar social or educational backgrounds tend to back away from the uncompromising stand that lies behind his smile; they do not believe in fairies. His Inkling friends did not really either, not as Tolkien himself believed in them. Tolkien can be embarrassing with his truth, always an unwelcome bounty to deliver; the most trying things may be in it. The children and those who cherish simplicity, the hippies and the wooden-beads-and-sandals set, in whom he has aroused enthusiasm, are far away from sharing in the attraction among the turbulent college set, faculty as well as student. This is a surprising cult, this campus trend, because Tolkien is all conservative, traditional and rigid, more uncompromising about blood, sweat and tears than Churchill ever was, although he says it more gracefully than that old bulldog. The campus crews are all on a Quest, certainly, but it is hard to believe they are following Tolkien's direction. Is it because they do not see Tolkien's way that they follow it, the poor bereft orphans who have no home? Maybe they would like to be Hobbits; if so, they were born too late: it's for Sauron or Strider now.

The land of Tolkien is in the present and the future as the time of Arthur, the once and future king, is. It's time to organize now, to form a Fellowship, or it will be too late. This is the last generation for a long time that will be free to drift, to look for causes. The lines are forming; the frantic scurry calls to mind the time before the final call: "Fall-In!"

The Hobbits Meriadoc, Pippin, Sam Gamgee, the squireen Bilbo and Frodo Baggins, heir to Bilbo, in whose veins runs the Took strain and that of the great Bull-Roarer, seem to be the real heroes of *The Lord of the Rings*, yet it is because they transcend their hobbitry that they win through; they grow up to be men. And if they, half-sized, furry feet and all, can do it, what can Man not do? questions Tolkien. It is Strider, the feudal knight of a Man, who shares Gandalf's great apprehension of the other evils that may come to harass earth after the power of the Lord of the Rings has been destroyed and the contemporary evil of Sauron flung back into the dark. But it's a Hobbit who saves the Kingdom.

Other evils there are that may come, for Sauron is himself but a servant or emissary. Yet it is not our part to master all the tides of the world, but to do what is in us for the succour of these years wherein we are set.

It is around the Hobbits, however unwillingly separate from their humdrum and bucolic home, that the forces of Right stand around about, nearly all above them in estate and none below them. Victory requires them; without them there can be none. Defeat is sure if it is left to a few quixotic knights to combat Evil. Man must share in his own redemption.

The most pitiable foe is not the most powerful, the dark

89

Sauron, who matches and combats the guile of the guide of the Right, Gandalf, the one good wizard, but Gollum, who has lost his innocence and all that might have been a pleasant Hobbit life through madness, a madness that came upon him through a craving that was kindled and fired into him from beyond his ken. Gollum is a very subtle creation of Tolkien, who is nearly ruined by the slobber of speech Tolkien gives him. Slobber there must be, and it is beyond anyone but Tolkien to better it, but it is hard to hear. Yet, after all, the whole affair of Gollum is hard to take; that is how true it is.

Gollum once was of the Hobbit kind; Smeagol was his name. There is the very mystery of Damnation in the poor wretch. His plight contains the whole crux of the theological matter and of Tolkien's. Smeagol falls, is plunged into Hell, and not of his own volition. The weakness that the Ring bared in Gollum was bared in all the others too, but good company and rearing, a part of the human condition, saved them. Still temptation, when it damns Gollum, seems like predestination, worse even than blind chance. The presence of Grace did not operate for that poor thing. Grace imposes an order on the Universe, an Order seen in Tolkien as operating with little apparent consolation and falling where it lists, avoiding and thereby damning Gollum.

The greatest consolation of all, the Grace to pursue and combat evil, to have the power to strive and to prevail, out of free will and choice, is a grace given to few, and then mainly because of the good their past, their ancestors, has stored up for them. Tolkien's Hobbits, barring Gollum, an ex-Hobbit, if ever there can be an ex-Hobbit any more than an ex-Man, are redeemed, by this Grace, made good enough to challenge and halt the very Devil and in good company to be friends.

There are haunts and glories on Tolkien's earth, sacrifice and failing too. The scenes of battle could not have been written by a non-soldier, the storm-swept crossing of a snowy mountain by one who could not have been there in the flesh. Every writer is bound by his experience and by those other things that he might not have experienced but is capable of experiencing. This goes for Love and Hate, Courage and Disaster, as well as for the more mundane matters. Real humor is so hard to write and come by; tales of family life even more so.

An abiding lesson of Tolkien, one that has not been developed nearly enough, is that Time is against Man, is on the side of Evil. Always, every time until now, the soldier returns from the wars and hangs up his gun, relishes his ease, takes his comfort before the fire and revives his life domestic. He has done his part in making the world free, so now he joins the Legion, presses for pensions, seeks for the easy indolent way, puts some money in the plate and buys some Salvation-Church building bonds. He seeks for security and the happy life. The soldiers are already in the thrall of the Ring Lord they defeated. They trim, exercise prudent judgment, wheel and deal. They start to operate, keep up with the neighbors; the tides of Man are on the ebb again. The zeal, courage and optimism of wartime degenerate into opportunism during times of peace.

Tolkien's war will never be over as long as there is life. Conflict is the heart of life. There are always the Powers sapping at the walls; Time disarms Man's guard. Strife to the bitter end is Man's lot, which he evades like a bush runner, and Time beguiles, being on the side of the Enemy. Outside, with Time on his side, Dark is creeping in again, nearer every day that Man neglects the debt he owes the earth that has saved and nourished him with flowers and fruit, stayed him with Hobbits. The blanket of the Dark weaves itself with only one purpose in mind: to cover the Light. The Light dances in the sum, slumbers and muses over beauty, becomes the victim and the prey again of Evil, until heroism is needed once again, so men go and die, exert themselves to their own death to stop the Universal Death. Then, every time yet, they return, the few who are left whole, and dream of a timeless Haven on his earth, of a Never-Never-Land. Once Man is born, Time starts taking toll. The toll increases with every day of Life, until Time calls for the checkout and Man dies of it.

That is the lot of human kind; Tolkien tells it. The Elvish tongue, the Inkling company and interest and his children may have brought Tolkien to this chronicle, but, above all, through all its wonders and contrived beauty, it is a call to arms, a harsh and inexorable call to arms. Wherever there is green, sky, sea and sun and good remaining, Time is running out and bringing in the Dark, that is what the bugle of the book brays.

Tolkien reveals that this danger, Man's never ending dilemma, can never be too clearly seen in the present, because of the dirty distractions of the world. The present is too much with us. Lord of the world, Man is beguiled by its transient beauty, nearly all of him forgets the danger, is bewildered and delighted by the bawdy and the bustle of it. Man never clearly sees himself or those around him who are of his bosom, his wife and children, let alone his friends, the folk of his land, the people of his world, even when he can understand their tongue. The vision he enjoys of this world is cloven from the truth. It needs Fantasy to free men's vision. Chesterton frees it in his story of the mailman, when he describes him so clearly that he is seen for the first time, when it is too late to do anything about it.

CHAPTER X

EPILOGUE

Fantasy is based on hard fact. Lewis Carroll based his fantasy on his mathematical logic; it is required reading for students in that discipline. "Fantasy is a natural human activity . . . the better and the clearer is the reason, the better fantasy it will make." Tolkien expounded this absurd truth in his Andrew Lang lecture. All fantastic elements in prose and verse help to make a more sensible relation of the present to the abiding reality that governs all of Time. The fairy story, as in *The Lord of the Rings*, is the very core of Fantasy. There is wonder in it, a wonder compounded because it shows things as they really are. Every word comes alive. Tolkien, through the fairy story, discovered for himself at length the power of the Word.

He realized the wonder of things such as stone, wood, iron, bread and wine, things that are taken for granted, as current events make Man callous to the cutting down of a tree, to the decay to the City, to birth and death.

Rooted in the past so deeply that the origins lie beyond Man's ken, the fairy story offers an Escape, a guerdon that Tolkien awards this form of literary art. Escape has an ugly connotation in these days, betokening Surrender, Lotus Eating, Suicide. Tolkien queries this connotation, which makes dodgers of Pilgrim Fathers of Ulysses even. Why should a man incarcerated not want to escape, to go home? The Escape of the Prisoner is a far cry from the Flight of the Deserter. Fantasy is concerned more with the power of Lightning than with the wattage of street lamps; Light is of more fundamental importance than study lamps or fluorescent signs, which are not Light at all. The roof of an airport is real to all, but less of a roof, far, far less than the dome of the sky, is the roof over the world that contains the vaulting enterprise of the fairy story. The present artifacts, clothing and times, with all the power that heralds and extols their status importance, the non-real need for them, clamor for the attention and the energy of Man, who should be left alone a while to contemplate the eternity that will envelop him, free him from Mortality that so controls his thought and actions. The mind of Man, to be able to contemplate, must be refreshed and consoled by the Escape of Fantasy, to observe with more objectivity the greed, the panacea of carnality that the present dins in, day by day, every waking hour.

The Consolation of the fairy story above all is freedom, Escape from Death and worse, freedom from the fear of it. Since this Death of the body is inescapable for Man's condition, Tolkien suggests that fairy story be concerned with the Escape from Deathlessness: a saving and a seminal reflection. There is something terrifying about non-Death, which is not the same as Eternal life and may be Hell, but this condition of aimlessness, of no dimension, does prevail, even on this earth. And Death here or in the hereafter may be a solution, the Happy End. The fairy story must have that necessary Happy Ending or it would not true to its genre. Since there is no word to describe this highest function of the fairy story, Tolkien invents the clumsy word "eucatastrophe"—the good catastrophe. This Consolation depends upon the mystery of Grace; it denies the certainty, final and irrevocable defeat, and even permits a joy never to be counted on: evangelium, "Joy beyond the walls of the world, poignant as grief." This is the joy that on occasion, never the same, never to be counted on, "rends the very web of the story and lets a gleam come through."

Joy in Fantasy is a glimpse of basic truth, a satisfaction as well as a consolation, according to the canon of Tolkien. When the truth of a fairy story breaks in on Man, brings him the primary truth he longs for, hopes for, wishes he could believe in: Ressurection.

For every good Tolkien reveals, there is a corresponding evil. Saruman the fallen wizard is the counterpart to Gandalf the good, the Grey. The Strider, Aragorn the King, has his opposite in the frenzied Steward of Minas Tirith, Denethor, and Frodo has the wretched erstwhile Hobbit, Gollum.

The exactitude with which Tolkien invests his story has a certain sanctity in it, a law, above all. It appeals to Man and is accepted or angrily rejected, depending on the individual's nature wherein, again, Grace is at work, one way or the other. This is the Vision that is implicit in the subcreation, something spiritual in Man's desire to hear the horns of Elfland sound, however far away. Tolkien sounds this to those who would hear; it is up to them to cock the ear.

Tolkien creates a very melody in the words he uses for his persons, places and things. To read the Index alone gives a sense of pleasure in the very sound: Anarion and Appledore, Aragorn and Arriven, Baramir, Bombadil and Butterbur, Denethor and Dúnedain, Elberth and Ents, Fallohide and Findulais, Quickbeam and Shadowfax, Tinuviel and Treebeard—hundreds of words he has fabricated or created, mainly from the Celtic Welsh or the Norse.

He adds a style of narrative to these words, a dialogue that suits admirably the persons involved, save in the light comedy of the Hobbits' parlance, when his love, his particular youthful predilection, breaks through, good enough to command some affection and understanding of the Inklings, but far below the universal style of most of his writing.

The fantastic and involved tale of Tolkien that has aroused so much interest, not only in the world of English, but in other tongues, too, proves that he chanced, or came upon through his lore, a universal need to relate. The Tolkien relation is not so well understood as the legend of Prometheus, with its bearing on these days, nor will his work ever be; it is too voluminous and lacks the traditional interpretations of the Greek. The Greek myths form the theme of much creative writing these days, and there is warning and despair in them for Man, when left to his own devices; this gloomy note is never found in Tolkien.

Tolkien is the bearer of a promise that can be more desired because it is within Man's own grasp. It's a myth that he has propounded, but one that carries within it the promise of the morning, when the sun will break through and be again what it was before, the warmth and welcome of good news, the everlasting light that dispels the darkness and shows Man's way clear to his final ending after earth—if he's worth it—to Lothlórien when he has shouldered arms here on earth and Sergeant Death has stacked them as he falls. Then words like Tolkien's will rise up in songs of greeting. Words that will tell of the Kingdom where there will be no end, nothing save that of Man's own desiring.

Tolkien's relation is all in his writing, even if he did not know it was coming through so plain. He is vigorous and lively still but has the sign of a man who has been through it. He has suffered for his opinions and shows it, though he may deny it. His conservative beliefs extend far beyond his writing into life, and he roundly proclaims himself an arch-believer in all that is tried and tested and good, decrying just as strongly all the tentative and violent efforts of these days to break away from the past. He loves England for what it used to be for him, not for its present trends. Laughter comes easily to him, and he can sing out loudly and confidently, with relish, the Elvish liturgy of Middle-earth. He can trip out lyrics for Michael Flanders and Donald Swann, slap his knee with gusto when he recalls that a baritone who might sing this liturgy, set to a sort of Gregorian chant, is named Elvin. Tolkien can grasp a hand in greeting, perch forward on a chair in his crowded garage of a study and remember Roy Campbell so vividly that the poet seems to be but around the corner, marching up the London Road.

Most of the Trilogy, all of it maybe, was written in the city of Oxford, in Merton or Exeter, or in Holywell, in his study at home. There the sound and the smell of Oxford, now for decades compounded with an automobile roar, were around him as he worked. His home now, on Headington Hill, stands in a quiet sidestreet off the London Road, overlooking the Sacred Town, peaceful and serene enough when school is in session or when there is no soccer game in the neighboring field.

Oxford is changing now. The rising graduate schools and government commissions threaten its old order; it is engulfed in traffic. Dons commute farther and farther to work, hurry home at night to suburbs and houses in the country. The older ones proceed as if things were the same as ever, as they will be for as long as they are around. Tolkien sees the ending of this old order and goes with it. His work would not be the same, nor as good either, if he agreed with the changing times. Only a man of his background and beliefs could have written *The Lord of the Rings* seriously and through his own limitations, imposed by time. The book is the masterpiece of imaginative and spiritual literature.

Tolkien has worn well through the years. He looks like an older don in harness rather than one put out to pasture years ago. Those who listened to him years ago would have no difficulty in seeing in him as he is at present the strong young teacher of generations gone. This book about him will not please him, nor is it meant to. It is no bouquet, but it's not a brickbat either. It is only one man's view of him and his relation. Tolkien's work is great; its flaws help to make it a unique contribution to English literature. I dedicate this book to him.